D1329285

The testimonies in this book were compiled by the organisation Peace and Hope and originally published in Spanish with the support of Open Doors. The English version was translated with the assistance of CSW volunteers and edited by Anna Lee Stangl of Christian Solidarity Worldwide.

# CHRISTIAN SOLIDARITY WORLDWIDE

Christian Solidarity Worldwide is a human rights charity working all over the world on behalf of those who suffer repression. We promote religious liberty for all, with a special focus on the 250 million Christians persecuted for their faith worldwide.

CSW works all over the world . . .

- for *individual prisoners of conscience* like Irene Fernandes awaiting trial in Malaysia for her exposure of human rights abuses, and those *falsely accused* of terrorism in Peru
- for *legislation that adheres to universal standards of religious freedom* such as in Central Asia where registration requirements have denied many their freedom to worship
- for *innocent civilians caught in the crossfire of conflict* such as in Indonesia, Sudan and Nigeria
- for *children in need* such as those in Russia where we operate a pioneering child foster care programme

CSW works to highlight these injustices through raising awareness, campaigning and advocacy. Our publications provide first-hand reports from over 30 countries worldwide, and our supporters are equipped to pray and to write campaign letters to strategic decision makers. Supporters also send cards and letters of encouragement to those in prison. Our staff based in Westminster and Brussels ensure that CSW briefings and urgent appeals reach key officials in the European institutions and foreign ministries as well as the British government. In addition CSW advocacy targets other governments and multi-laterals organisations including the United Nations. Where resources allow, CSW provides humanitarian assistance to those in need.

*Proverbs 31:8 "Speak up for those who cannot speak for themselves."*

Christian Solidarity Worldwide
PO Box 99
New Malden
Surrey
KT3 3YF

# Tried by Fire

*Testimonies of courage and hope from Peru's Christian prisoners*

*Edited and translated by*
ANNA LEE STANGL

with the support of
CSW volunteers

*Compiled by*
PEACE AND HOPE

MONARCH
B O O K S

Mill Hill, London & Grand Rapids, Michigan

First published by Monarch Books in the UK 2003,
Concorde House, Grenville Place,
Mill Hill, London, NW7 3SA.

Published in the USA by Monarch Books 2004.

Published in conjunction with
Chrisitan Solidarity Worldwide

Distributed by:
UK: STL, PO Box 300, Kingstown Broadway, Carlisle,
Cumbria CA3 0QS;
USA: Kregel Publications, PO Box 2607,
Grand Rapids, Michigan 49501.

ISBN 1 85424 638 0 (UK)
ISBN 0 8254 6236 3 (USA)

**British Library Cataloguing Data**
A catalogue record for this book is available
from the British Library.

Book design and production for the publishers by
Bookprint Creative Services
P.O. Box 827, BN21 3YJ, England.
Printed in Great Britain.

# CONTENTS

# PREFACE
## Anna Lee Stangl

I visited Peru for the first time in March 2000. Terrorism had been virtually wiped out. It seemed that the country was just about to get back on its feet, and with the upcoming elections there was a general sense of optimism that Peru was entering a new era.

At the same time, however, this sense of hopefulness had not spread to the prisons. While some of their fellow inmates had been pardoned and released, hundreds more innocent men and women continued to be imprisoned in appalling conditions. The corrupt and dictatorial government that had put them there was still hanging on to power. Hope remained, however, in the form of two tiny Christian charities, one Catholic, one Protestant, which were bravely waging a battle for justice.

I have returned each year since that visit, with Christian Solidarity Worldwide and have always come away deeply impressed by the men and women I have met there – both inside and outside the prisons. Their strength of character and their undying faith in a just and loving God both amazes and challenges me. Each time I have the chance to listen to stories like those shared in this book it provokes me to consider, "Would I react this way?" Could I continue to trust in a loving and personal God in the face of such injustice and brutality? Or would I, in the words of Job's wife, prefer to "curse God and die"?

The following stories are personal testaments not only to the faithfulness of God to his children but also to the rewards of remaining faithful to him in the face of despair. Through their ordeal, each one of these men and women found a truer personal understanding of God's power, love, and protection. They emerged from their experience not broken down or bitter, but stronger and more convinced than ever of the reality of Christ's love. God sent each of these men and women into torture chambers and prison cells to bring his light and his redeeming power into the darkness of prison and to transform the lives of hundreds of other men and women who truly were the despised and forgotten of society and, regrettably, even disregarded by many in the church.

The men and women I have met, both those who have been released and those who still suffer inside prison, have shown me what real prayer is – and what it means to put all of one's hope in God without reservation. Choosing hope when logic tells you hope is useless can be a terrifying thing to do, as it leaves open the possibility for disappointment. I have to admit I often personally struggle to comprehend how some of these men and women cling to hope and their faith even after ten years without, it seems, any answer from God.

At the same time, I personally witness miracles every time I return to Peru. Each year that I go back I meet these answers to prayer in person – men and women I met the previous year inside prison, now freed and reunited with their families. During my first visit to Peru I was escorted into the prisons by Peace and Hope lawyer Wuille Ruiz Figueroa, who himself had been freed only two years before. He introduced me to Julio Cusihuaman Ccorahua – a prisoner and prison minister in Yanamilla Prison in Ayacucho. Julio's face, smiling out at us and blessing us from behind the prison bars as we went back out into freedom, is etched in my memory. The following year I returned to visit that same prison, accompanied this time by Julio and his little daughter, Candy – now united in freedom!

The dramatic downfall of the government that put them in prison in the first place was an answer to prayer that few had anticipated or could even have imagined, least of all me!

It is impossible for me to understand entirely the agony of torture or the pain of years of forced separation from my own family without undergoing it myself – but the fraction that I can begin to understand terrifies me. Every time I visit the prisons I am asked to pray or to share a Christian message, and each time this happens I am overwhelmed by a sense of my own total inadequacy. I have seen a light and a hope radiating from inside the dark, damp prison cells of Peru that I have rarely seen in a "free" church. I have been the recipient of immense Christian generosity and hospitality from prisoners, who invited me to eat the precious food their impoverished family had brought for them on their weekly visit. I have heard the true sound of joy in the singing voices of prisoners who have no rational reason to be joyful. I have heard words of hope uttered in an impossible situation that convicted me of my own puny faith. Paradoxically, it is by going into these prisons that I am reminded what freedom really is.

Anna Lee Stangl
Christian Solidarity Worldwide
13th June 2003

"Why are you taking me? Where are you taking me?" I asked.

Without answering he blindfolded me and made me get into a car. The confusion of the moment slowed me down; in response, a policeman dealt me a blow to the back of the neck.

This is how the interrogations and mistreatment began.

"Now you know why we've brought you here, don't you?" one of them asked.

"No, I don't know, but I'm ready to cooperate because I'm innocent," I responded.

Another policeman took out some papers and said, "Here we have the scientific proof that you belong to the Shining Path."

"I don't know what you're talking about. You must be wrong. Why don't you go over it again – check it out more thoroughly? Do a better job than you've been doing? I'm not a terrorist," I replied.

This infuriated them and they began to beat me.

At first I received only blows. When I tried to cover myself I would receive yet another blow. Full of anger, they beat me on the face and the stomach. The beating was endless. One particularly violent punch under my chest left me with a broken rib. I begged them to stop but they threw me to the floor. After this blow, the hood they had placed over my head came off, and I recognised one of them as Captain Tello. The punches and blows were continuous.

After a few minutes I spoke out. "I am a believer in Jesus Christ; I'm a Christian; I'm not a terrorist and what you are doing to me is unjust. We have a just God and it is he who will bring justice."

"I'm also a Christian," yelled one of the policemen, "and God is going to congratulate me because you are a criminal. You are part of the group that has been doing so much damage to society."

# INTRODUCTION
## Alfonso Wieland

How do the testimonies of people who have suffered unjust imprisonment help us? Is it possible to find anything edifying or uplifting as we learn about the lives of men and women plagued by misfortune, who have fallen victim to the absurdity that is called "justice"? What purpose does it serve to rehash the past, a past rife with violence that many Peruvians themselves would not wish to remember?

Because, generally, victims of injustice do not have a voice and the public has a very short memory, their ordeals run the risk of falling into oblivion. This does not mean, however, that their suffering should not be significant for the rest of the population. It is for this reason that these stories can tell us so much about who we are as a people – what we do and what we neglect to do as a society. Above all else, these are stories of "anonymous heroes", tried by fire, sentenced to darkness, whose faith in the God of Truth was dramatically changed during this epoch of their lives. Although they have now been freed, the message that their stories hold for us should not be overlooked.

It is essential that we understand that justice is not only

God's concern, but is actually part of our own nature. All injustice is an assault on God and on his majesty and glory. As we Christians call ourselves children of this God, we cannot fail to react when the dignity of a person is demeaned. This is not an option for us; it is an obligation that is central to our faith. We neglect the responsibility that comes along with being a child of God when we fail to pursue justice for our persecuted brothers and sisters. What does Jehovah ask of you? (Micah 6:8)

The peace of a nation cannot have its foundation built on the pain and suffering of its most vulnerable. Perhaps this may prove successful in the short term, but the cancer will continue to grow under the crust of society. Fighting terror by terrorising the innocent is not only the wrong answer, but is also immoral. The good news is that it is never too late to invite justice to rule over our villages and towns. Christ is the door through which we can seek to pursue justice.

Trial by fire, undergone by those who believe in a real and living God, is not a reason for shame but rather the opposite: it is a reaffirmation of their dignity and their identity. These testimonies speak to us of people who learned to rise above the pain. They testify to a miracle of spiritual liberation and the discovery of new dimensions to their faith. They learned to depend completely upon God and to do good even as evil was done to them. They were not consumed by hatred and rancour towards their enemies; they learned the true meaning of forgiving them. They learned not to fear those who can only destroy the body. This is the fruit of the Spirit of Christ that manifests itself in his followers.

It is incredible to comprehend how a prison could serve as the hallowed site of a mission, also under God's dominion. Perhaps it has something to do with the promise that the darkness can never overcome the light. At the same time we should not idealise our prisons, however, as they continue to be a festering wound, demanding decisive action on the part of society and the church.

As we read these testimonies, we are touched with a reverent awe of a God who cares for his own. His care, however, does not always mean an absence of suffering. It is principally a real and spiritual victory over the fear of death, corruption, squalor and the unbalanced indignity that sometimes passes for justice. In no way should this provide a bit of abstract advice, a psychological escape or a loss of reason. This is about FAITH, in capital letters. Faith in that which we cannot see, in the reward of eternal life; faith to understand the truth of his testimony although we do not see the fulfilment of his promises here, and faith in a Teacher who suffered much more than any of us.

It is important to look into the mirror of the suffering and victory of this handful of witnesses to the justice of God. In doing so we recognise that we are all part of the same family of faith, but, more importantly, we come to know ourselves even better – not with the objective of making us feel guilty but rather to make us better citizens, better men and women, better children of God. And, if we are better sons and daughters of the Creator, then we become messengers and builders of justice in a generation that is thirsty for life.

We conclude by thanking all of those people through whom the Spanish version of this book was made possible: Rolando Perez and German Vargas. Together with them, Jhonny Lleerna, who helped with the editing and text style. We would like to offer our particular gratitude to Open Doors for their work in fanning the bonfire of faith, making it possible to set alight the testimonies of lives that were tried by fire. And of course, special thanks to Christian Solidarity Worldwide and Tearfund from the UK and Solidaridad and ICCO from

Holland. They all have been real partners in this battle for justice for the poor.

Alfonso Wieland, Director, Peace and Hope
Lima, December 1999

# HISTORY

While the plight of the disappeared and murdered in the "Dirty Wars" of the 1970s and 1980s in Argentina and Chile have received international attention, the internal war in Peru that led to the murder or disappearance of more than 60,000 people in the 1980s and 1990s, though more recent, is less well known.

Beginning in the early 1980s, the Shining Path, a radical guerrilla group, started a terrorist campaign in an effort to bring about a new social order in Peru. Under the guidance of a university professor by the name of Abimael Guzman, they based their principles on Maoist philosophy. Like the Khmer Rouge in Cambodia they singled out the "privileged" for elimination. This term included all types of leaders – from major government figures to village teachers and priests, traditional community leaders, and landowners. In addition, their form of Maoism was militantly atheist, which meant that Christians, and particularly church leaders, were special targets.

One of the Shining Path's basic convictions was that 15 per cent of the population had to die in order to create enough instability to allow them to usher in a new social system.

Peru's mountainous topography meant that provincial villages and cities were often left with absolutely no security support from the state. The guerrillas, who were heavily armed themselves because of cooperation agreements with cocaine and heroin traffickers, often outmatched local police and military patrols. Massacres of civilians took place week after week.

From 1980 to 1990 the violence increased and the terror began to spread from the provinces to the cities. Many of the *campesinos*, or peasants, fled en masse to the cities, particularly Lima, in an effort to escape the insecurity of the provinces. The guerrillas followed them, however, infiltrating the shanty towns that sprang up around Lima.

A favourite tactic of the guerrillas was to blow up one of the city's power stations, cutting off the electricity to entire neighbourhoods and plunging them into darkness. The dark, which was often more than enough to terrify the inhabitants, was then used as a cover for terrorist operations, which usually involved more bloodshed. The attacks in Lima became more and more frequent. As the city is the centre of Peruvian government and wealth, this put the ruling élite into a panic.

In the meantime, the military had stepped up its operations around the country. Military officers operated with virtual impunity as they arbitrarily detained civilians, torturing them and often murdering or "disappearing" them. Their tactics were often indistinguishable from those of the terrorists, which left ordinary men and women trapped in a vice-grip of violence. There was, literally, no one to turn to. In one highland town villagers were told by the military that they should keep their doors open to prove they had nothing to hide – a closed door meant they were terrorists. At the same time, the Shining Path made it clear that an open door would be considered a sign of collaboration with the government and that they should keep them closed if they valued their lives. Open or closed? This was the life or death quandary in which Peruvians across the country found themselves living from day to day.

The church, both Protestant and Roman Catholic, was also caught in the middle. Many Christians wanted no part in the conflict and attempted to stay neutral. In the eyes of the Shining Path and the military, however, neutrality was not an option. Non-participation equalled disloyalty and disloyalty had severe consequences – usually bloodshed. The violence touched the church at its heart, as not only were individual priests and pastors murdered but entire congregations fell victim to atrocities committed by both the guerrillas and the military.

This was the chaotic stage onto which Alberto Fujimori stepped after he was elected president of Peru in 1990. He promised a terrified population that the rebels' attack on the nation would be brought to a definitive end, and he went straight to work. He suspended the constitution and shut down Congress and the judiciary. The military stepped up their anti-terrorism campaign across the country and Fujimori gave them free reign to do so. In 1995, in fact, he granted a general amnesty to all military personnel for all human rights abuses committed after 1980 and through the 1990s. This sent a message that there would be no repercussions for any of the atrocities, past and future, that they committed against civilians. Reports of arbitrary detention, torture and forced disappearances at the hands of government security agents soared.

Fujimori's next step was the instalment of a system of "faceless judges". These judges anonymously tried and sentenced thousands of Peruvians on charges of treason and terrorism. Men and women were unexpectedly plucked out of their homes by the military or the police, often at the dead of night.

They were tortured, and given a trial that frequently lasted no more than fifteen or twenty minutes. They were rarely allowed to have a lawyer and they were not allowed to cross-examine witnesses, challenge government evidence or give testimony in their own defence. Most were sentenced to upwards of 20 years in prison by a judge they never even saw. A large proportion of them were completely innocent. Their number included both men and women: students, farmers, teachers, young and old, fathers and mothers, even teenagers. Many of them were Christians.

Rather than allowing the injustice of their situation to make them bitter or cynical, many of the wrongly imprisoned Christians decided to use this as an opportunity to reach out to the other inmates. Former terrorists and narco-traffickers have come to Christ inside the prisons of Peru because of these faithful men and women. Catholics and Protestants work together in harmony in many of the prisons and they consider themselves to be a united Christian community. These communities have continued to grow within the confines of the prison and are a real ministry in and of themselves.

Because of their exemplary behaviour and also through the efforts of Peace and Hope and CEAS (the Catholic Episcopal Commission for Social Action), many of these Christian groups have been granted a special freedom of movement and privileges not enjoyed by other prisoners who are still considered high-risk. In certain prisons a cellblock may be set aside for Christian communities, with the doors remaining unlocked, permitting the prisoners to move around freely for Bible studies and prayer and worship meetings. They may also be allowed to keep tools and crafts and hold outreaches.

Historically in Peru the church had not been known for speaking out as an entity on political topics. However, in the mid-1980s both the National Evangelical Council (CONEP) and the Roman Catholic Church under the auspices of CEAS began to receive more and more reports of wrongful imprisonment. They sent out lawyers and social workers to the prisons to interview prisoners – many of whom had never received any legal support whatsoever. These two organisations, along with a number of others, began to put pressure on the Peruvian government to admit that mistakes had been made.

The result of their efforts was a three-man Ad Hoc Commission for Pardons, set up in August 1996 to review the hundreds of cases of men and women who claimed to be wrongly imprisoned. Peace and Hope and CEAS, along with other organisations, used this opportunity to submit a number of cases for consideration. Their efforts were backed up by international organisations such as Christian Solidarity Worldwide, Tearfund and Open Doors, who brought news about these men and women to Christians around the world. They in turn began to pray for them and write letters to them and their families to offer them encouragement in the midst of their ordeal.

While many prisoners benefited from the pardoning scheme, they were not actually able to be released from prison until Fujimori put his personal signature onto each recommendation for pardon issued by the Commission. Fujimori did sign some of them, but between December 1998 and July 2000 he frustrated the process by refusing to sign any release documents for prisoners who had already been found innocent by the Ad Hoc Commission, leaving them stranded inside the prisons.

Fujimori attempted to hang on to power after internationally condemned elections in the first half of 2000. Many observers both inside and outside Peru feared that he now had an unshakeable hold on power. Over the course of his two terms in office he had rewritten the Peruvian constitution, giving himself almost dictatorial power over the rest of the country.

However it was Fujimori's own dishonesty that led to his downfall in the autumn of 2000. By September of that year journalists discovered that a huge number of legislators, judges, military officers and even narco-traffickers had been bribed and blackmailed into supporting Fujimori. It became clear that, with the shadowy assistance of the National Intelligence Service head, Vladimir Montesinos, who was also responsible for the anti-terrorism campaign, Fujimori had established a web of corruption that penetrated all aspects of Peruvian government, society and the military. The Peruvian Congress voted to remove him from office and Fujimori went into self-imposed exile in Japan.

The end of the year 2000 was a turning point for Peru. Now that Fujimori had been removed from office, a web of corruption and a systematic disregard for human rights were brought out into the open. For the first time in years, hundreds of innocent men and women who remained in prison had new hope that their cases might receive a fair review. Under the interim government in the first half of 2001 their plight was made a priority. During that period, more than 70 men and women were found to have been wrongly convicted, and were pardoned and released. Many had spent a decade in prison – separated from their family and loved ones – for a crime they did not commit. In addition, a Truth and Reconciliation Commission was set up, charged with investigating human-rights atrocities committed by both the government and guerrilla groups throughout the violent years.

Dr Alejandro Toledo was democratically elected as president and took office on 28th July, 2001. In the first year of his presidency he signed the release papers of a number of wrongly convicted prisoners. At the beginning of 2002 he took the enormously significant step of offering a personal official apology on behalf of the nation to all 726 wrongfully imprisoned men and women who had received pardons and been released. He also promised that almost 2,000 pending applications would be reviewed. Perhaps most importantly, President Toledo announced the creation of a special commission to investigate the possibility of non-monetary reparations to the victims of wrongful imprisonment on charges of terrorism and treason.

In July 2002 President Toledo also promised to overhaul the anti-terrorist laws that had put these people in prison in the first place. In December 2002, the Constitutional Tribunal found the anti-terrorism laws to be unconstitutional – and the government is now in the process of reforming the laws without inadvertently releasing any real terrorists.

As 2002 went on, however, his willingness to follow up on these commitments was called into question. After signing the pardons of eleven men and women in March, he neglected to sign the pardons of seventeen more, found innocent by the Ministry of Justice in late spring, until October 2002 (following an international campaign for their releases). There was no explanation given for the almost six-month delay, which caused enormous stress and anxiety to the prisoners and their families. They knew they had been found innocent – but they were not allowed to leave the prison.

Although the overall situation in Peru has improved, it is still fairly unstable. Poverty continues to be a massive problem across the country, and unemployment exists on a large scale. The instability has allowed some of the terrorist groups to resume their activity, though on a much smaller scale, in remote parts of the country, and it remains to be seen how dedicated the government really is to eliminating corruption and upholding human rights. In the meantime, innocent men and women still await justice in Peruvian prisons and thousands more await the truth of what happened to their disappeared and murdered loved ones. It provides an opportunity for the church – not only in Peru but in the rest of Latin America and in the world – to fulfil its prophetic role

> to loose the chains of injustice
> and untie the cords of the yoke,
> to set the oppressed free
> and break every yoke.

# CHAPTER ONE

# JUAN

The civil war in Peru began in 1980 with the uprising by the Shining Path. It included forced disappearances, torture and horrific murders, not only on the part of the subversive groups but also carried out by the paramilitary "commandos" supported by the forces of "order", as part of a strategy to stamp out the Shining Path.

In the later years, one of these commando units, the Colina Group, began to commit some of the most serious human-rights violations. Two of their most infamous crimes were carried out in Lima. The first was in Barrios Altos in November 1991, where they fired blindly upon a crowd of 20 people celebrating a *pollada* – a fundraiser to improve the decrepit sewage system. The majority were ice-cream vendors and other street merchants. Fifteen of them died, among them a child only eight years of age.

The other crime was committed in July 1992 at the Enrique Gusman y Valle National University (La Cantuta), near Lima. After breaking into a student residence they abducted and murdered nine students and one professor.

This last crime was uncovered with the help of a secret

group of army officers, who were unhappy with the level of corruption in their institution and with the presence of mercenaries in its interior. These officers denounced the Colina Group as the perpetrators of the crime, commited under the direction of Major Santiago Martín Rivas, who took power with support from the highest military levels. The denunciation included Vladimiro Montesinos, presidential consultant and the man in charge of the National Intelligence Service. This same group of officers submitted a manuscript to the *Revista Si* with directions on how to find the graves where the remains of the murdered students and professor were buried.

The government tried a number of different strategies to demonstrate that these Death Commandos did not exist. A few members of parliament developed their own explanations, for example Congressman Gilberto Siura, the author of the thesis of "self-abduction".

The other strategy of the government was to blame the Shining Path for the murders. But they lacked a scapegoat, and they found one in a humble taxi driver, Juan Malléa Tomaylla, who was accused of fabricating the paper that led the media to the graves.

After completing secondary school Juan had decided to enlist in the army, where he completed his military service in ten months. He was in the Rimac Force in Lima, where he suffered under the harsh regime of this military institution. Having finished secondary school he was awarded certain privileges by his superiors, but he still found himself forced to gain respect from others through blows. During the "False Paquisha" conflict with Ecuador, his entire unit travelled north to the border to repel the invasion from the neighbouring country.

In 1980, upon leaving the army, he found employment as assistant to an electrician and began his studies at the

Polytechnic Salesiano campus. Later he worked as an industrial electricity specialist for various businesses. In 1983 an accident at work left half of his body burnt. His case wasn't as grave as that of one of his colleagues, who became a human torch. Malléa considered it a divine miracle that he was spared more serious injury. It was at this time that he became involved with the Christian Missionary Alliance Church of Comas in the north part of Lima.

Juan continued working at various businesses, however he often had problems with his employers because they would not supply the necessary security devices to prevent accidents like the one he had already suffered. Discouraged by this, he opted to involve himself in a different sort of work.

When he reached 26 he acquired a job selling clothing in the Blue Flea Market (an open-air market of electronic equipment, clothing and other products set up along the edge of the government palace). This was a fruitful activity, allowing him to purchase a new car and many other luxuries. The business was profitable. Seven years later he married Maria Cristina, an evangelical from the Baptist Church, who, out of love for Juan, had begun to attend his church two years before they were married.

This period of his life was marked by an overall material well-being. At the same time, however, his spiritual life was plagued by difficulty. In the year of his marriage, 1992, Juan suffered a severe emotional blow. One of the brothers at his church, a member of the Aerea Force, was killed in a terrorist attack. His truck was attacked as he returned from shopping at the Parada Market. Five other soldiers were also killed. Juan, praying between sobs, thought, "What I wouldn't give to see these criminals face to face to rebuke them and bring them to account for the death of my dear friend. . . ."[1]

In 1993 a new drama began in the life of Juan and his

family. A huge fire engulfed the Blue Flea Market, where he had his stall. The fire began at dawn on the first of January, as all of Lima celebrated the New Year. The previous day had been a hugely busy shopping day, and as a result many of the vendors chose to leave the money from the sales of the day under guard at the stalls. The majority lost everything. Juan was also affected by this tragedy and it was during this time that he began to work as a taxi driver.

A month after the fire the engine in his car broke down. His finances were rapidly dwindling. He couldn't explain what was happening. In March, as he was working to repair his market stall, he fell and broke his right arm on the pavement. He had to wear a cast for three months. "What is going on, Lord? Why are you taking everything away from me?" he asked.

These were difficult months. Fortunately Maria Cristina worked as a teacher and her income met the needs of the family. In July of that year she received a bonus and decided to buy clothing for their son, Juanito. For some reason she bought a swathe of garment cloth and some toys. They didn't know why; they just knew they should do it.[2] One week later, on 10th July 1993, Juan Malléa was detained by the police.

In the following sections, he tells us what happened.

# I

It was the night of July 10th. I returned to the house after an entire day spent driving my taxi. I was tired and tense from the tumultuous atmosphere that permeated Lima: attacks, blackouts, car bombs and so much violence. All of a sudden a neighbour approached me. He demanded vehemently that I pick him up at dawn the next morning.

In this period my wife and I had a stall at the Blue Flea Market, where we sold clothing. Unfortunately, in January of this year, 1993, a huge fire swept through the market, affecting all of the merchants in the area. Many attempted to restore their stalls and this was exactly what I was doing when I had an accident that almost cost my life. I spent three months with a cast and without work. Afterwards, our premature son aged six months developed an acute infection. And, as if that wasn't enough, our family car, our last recourse, broke down. However, the love and mercy of our Father in heaven is so great that he allowed us to repair the car, which we were able to use as a taxi.

This was how we survived, with the taxi service that I provided. On July 10th, however, I had already committed myself to a friend for the next morning and I asked the neighbour to excuse me, but he insisted.

"But if it's on the way, what is the problem?" he said.

When he continued to insist that I take him, I finally agreed, on the condition that we leave at 4:00 am.

Just as I said, we left at dawn on July 11th. We were heading towards another zone in the same district of Comas. On the way, he had me turn off onto a side street and he asked me to wait there while he got something from a house there. Still sleepy, I had leaned back to doze in my seat when a voice awoke me.

"Get out of the car; it's the police!"

"What's happening? Is there a problem?" I began to ask.

"Just get out; don't wait until we force you to!"

Immediately they began to search through the interior of my car, but they found nothing. The only thing they did find was the Bible that I always took with me. From what they were saying I gathered that my neighbour had links with the subversive movement. Then I also noticed that the house we had stopped at had been surrounded and entered by DINCOTE (the national anti-terrorism directorate).

I tried to explain to them that I was just driving a taxi. I insisted that I had nothing whatsoever to do with terrorists.

"You are talking to the public prosecutor, sir," one of them cut me off abruptly. "And at this particular moment your attempts to defend yourself don't make very much sense!"

I invited them to come to my house to prove my innocence.

As we arrived, my parents met us, as surprised as I was.

"These men are from DINCOTE and they are just here to verify that I have nothing to do with terrorists," I said, trying to calm them down.

Upset at first, but more calm afterwards, my father himself showed them to the room where I slept. Later, attempting to relieve her worry, the public prosecutor told my wife, Cristina, "Calm down, madam. This is just an operation to prove the innocence of your husband; the man he drove this morning is a high-level leader of the Shining Path."

After going through all our belongings item by item, the only things they found were photos of our wedding and the church that we belonged to. After over an hour of questioning and searching they made us sign a record of the procedure.

"Don't worry, Mr Malléa," they told my father. "From what we see here, your son is innocent. He'll be released in two or three days and you won't have any more problems."

After these words they took me out. I was only able to take a coat to ward off the early morning chill. That day, Sunday 11th July, they were taking a population census of all of Peru. Because of this my family were unable to find out about my status until the following Monday. Days later I found out that my photograph had been published in a magazine along with the words, "The Shining Path Group That Authored *El Diario*

Meets its Downfall". (*El Diario* was a lampoon edited and published clandestinely.)

Upon arriving at DINCOTE, the situation suddenly changed.

"Look, no one gets out of here alive. You are going to spend at least fifteen days here while the investigation continues," said the police.

In this place the cells were one by one-and-a-half metres. Because of the overcrowding they put me in a cell with three or four other people. I spent fourteen days there.

I spent two days without seeing anybody outside the cell and without eating anything. The third day they brought me something to eat. I had to arm myself with serenity. Inside I had so many questions, but I never stopped trusting the Lord. In the midst of all this trouble, I was sure that he was my help. I understood even less after they placed me in the sector where all the prisoners accused of terrorism were held: I was now living side by side with the dreaded Shining Path.

At DINCOTE they had told my wife there would be a period of fifteen days before the investigation was complete. She tried to intercede for me, declaring my innocence, but all she received in return were humiliations and laughter. It was at the same office, however, that someone advised her to find a lawyer. They gave her an address and the name of a lawyer, Etel Villanueva.

When she found him, this lawyer after a clever but empty speech enthusiastically told her, "Your husband can be released today, madam, but this will cost 200 dollars, which must be paid up front."

My noble wife, desperate, took all of her wages, and, after converting them to dollars, gave them to the lawyer. This man never attended a hearing and never spoke with me.

After so much time behind bars, the cold nights and

mornings seemed endless. The day began with bloody torture. The temperature dipped down to zero. The loud music announced a concert of screams and heartrending weeping. We watched fearfully . . . after a few hours of this, a macabre parade: sad human figures with bloody faces returning, staggering, to their cells.

My body was covered with goosebumps; the cold invaded me. Overcome with anxiety, I thought that at any minute they would come for me – I told myself I would not stand for it.

Until my hour came. It was 2:00 in the morning on the 21st July. A cellmate woke me up and told me, "They're calling you. They're calling you to go to work."

"To work at this hour?" I said, surprised.

"Here, when they call you to work, it means the beatings are about to begin," he commented crudely.

They were going to torture me.

A policeman took me by the arm and shoved me out of the cell.

"Why are you taking me? Where are you taking me?" I asked.

Without answering he blindfolded me and made me get into a car. The confusion of the moment slowed me down; in response, a policeman dealt me a blow to the back of the neck.

This is how the interrogations and mistreatment began.

"Now you know why we've brought you here, don't you?" one of them asked.

"No, I don't know, but I'm ready to cooperate because I'm innocent," I responded.

Another policeman took out some papers and said, "Here we have the scientific proof that you belong to the Shining Path."

"I don't know what you're talking about. You must be wrong. Why don't you go over it again – check it out more thoroughly? Do a better job than you've been doing? I'm not a terrorist," I replied.

This infuriated them and they began to beat me.

At first I received only blows. When I tried to cover myself I would receive yet another blow. Full of anger, they beat me on the face and the stomach. The beating was endless. One particularly violent punch under my chest left me with a broken rib. I begged them to stop but they threw me to the floor. After this blow, the hood they had placed over my head came off, and I recognised one of them as Captain Tello. The punches and blows were continuous.

After a few minutes I spoke out. "I am a believer in Jesus Christ; I'm a Christian; I'm not a terrorist and what you are doing to me is unjust. We have a just God and it is he who will bring justice."

"I'm also a Christian," yelled one of the policemen, "and God is going to congratulate me because you are a criminal. You are part of the group that has been doing so much damage to society."

"Well, I don't know what kind of Christian you are. If you really understood what it meant to be a Christian you wouldn't be doing this," I said, trying to tone down his anger.

I could see that things were out of control. But, thanks to God, after these words of mine he calmed down considerably. The flood waters subsided. The torture had lasted approximately two hours.

I made my way back to my cell with difficulty and I began to pray. I said to the Lord, "God, I don't understand why this is happening to me. What is going on? Lord, forgive me for all that I've done wrong. I know that I've sinned, but give me the strength I need to get through this suffering."

The next day I found the strength to clean myself up. While I did so I tried to piece together my ideas about why all these things were happening to me. Even in this confusing environment I still had security, knowing that God was protecting me.

When I arrived at the prison there was already a group of fifteen people there who had been part of a military force. They had been sentenced to 30 years or to life. They always kept themselves at a distance from the common criminals.

One night, after obtaining a certain document, they became apprised of the individual crimes perpetrated by the other prisoners. In the manner of a celebration, they got everyone together to give their personal opinion on what was happening in the country. Each gave his or her point of view. I heard harsh critiques of the government and they talked about destroying the system.

And then it was my turn. I tried to maintain some human dignity and said, "The life of each one of us here has great value in the eyes of God. All of us are important to him. The truth is that I don't know how you can talk about destroying the system if each one of us is part of that system. We have to change the system; if the human being doesn't change himself, things will only continue to get worse."

Days later I was switched to another cell. There I met the two subversive groups, the Shining Path and Túpac Amaru. As the prison was overcrowded there was a great deal of friction between the two groups. They would fight over every piece of space.

Both groups ostracised the "independents". The Shining Path had plenty of space but didn't want to give it up.

One day, full of indignation, I stood up and said, "Why do you have to cause so many problems? What is your reason for not giving up a little space to the others here? Because they are weaker than you? What do you do with the weak?"

Happily, this appeased both sides.

One day I met another Christian in jail. His name was Daniel Aquije.

"How long have you known the Lord?" I asked him.

"Well, as you are part of the same spiritual family I can count on you with confidence," he said. "I always attended church, but when I was thirteen years old my mother died of cancer. This filled me with a profound sadness and I turned away from God. It was under these circumstances that I joined the ranks of the Shining Path."

When I suggested that he had probably joined under pressure, he replied that no, he hadn't. He had joined of his own volition and had worked up to become the head of a cell group.

"But all of that is now behind me; now I am a soldier of faith and I serve the Lord," he said, with a face full of confidence and security.

I confessed to him how much his story impressed me – that an ex-leader in the subversive movement now carried around his Bible and loved the Lord.

"You know," he said, "God has a plan in all of this, and this is an opportunity for us to speak to the rest of them about the blessing that comes with being children of God."

I had a beautiful friendship with Daniel. We prayed and read the Word together each day. Another prisoner, Simon Comborda, became part of our group. One day I remember I saw him looking so desperate that I asked him, "What's wrong, Simon? Calm yourself – we have to rest in the Lord."

"I know, brother, but it is so difficult. I'm worried about my children and my wife. Sometimes I think I'll be here all my life."

Simon was to share a cell with José Luis, a prisoner whom we didn't know. He was worried at first; he was afraid he would turn out to be a real criminal or worse. But when

Simon took out his Bible, he discovered that José Luis was also a Christian. Together they began to pray, and they embraced in joy. The next day Simon proposed that we pray each night to the Lord. Later, another prisoner (who was Catholic) joined us. Together we would conclude, "We give thanks to God for everything. We are going to praise him, praise him and nothing more." It was in this way that our group began.

In those days I met Segundo Pedro Hernandez Rojas. His was a story of terrible and painful experiences. I shared my faith with him. "We have to learn to trust and believe that we have a God who is just and who can help us. I have security in knowing that I have a God. Take refuge in him and he will begin to do many things."

These words consoled him.

One morning God directed me to one of the prisoners, who looked particularly desperate.

"Good morning. Can we talk? Can I help you somehow?"

"I don't think so," he answered me. "I don't have any way out. All of my family is in prison. No one visits me. I don't have a lawyer."

I gave him a sandwich that I had. "Take it; it's the only one I have."

"Thank you, friend. How kind you are."

"I just want you to know that there is a God, and Jesus Christ died on the cross for each one of us. All the things that we've done, all the wrongs that we've committed, have been washed away in the eyes of God," I told him.

Our experience with evangelism initially developed on a personal level, and the need to praise him together grew stronger. God also used people who were not Christians. We established a time to sing and read the Bible, "The Bible Hour". At various times I would begin to sing Joshua 1:9,

"Look . . ." Many fellow prisoners heard me and said to me, "Juan, we go around singing that 'valiant' song."

After a fair amount of time had passed, the same man asked me to come out in the hallway to read scripture. Many would listen in silence, but there was always somebody who would shout, "Listen, shut up, would you?"

I remember that days before my final day in DINCOTE, 23rd July, the police organised a press conference in order to present the captured Shining Path leaders to the public. Among them was the author of the paper on the graves at Cieneguilla. According to the police, this person was me. Before the conference, they took me out of my cell to sign an amplified version of my instructions. At about 11:00 in the morning the public prosecutor began to ask me new questions. I told him that I had been tortured.

"Who touched you?" he asked. "You'd better have proof before you say things like that."

"I can tell you who they are if I see them," I insisted.

Without answering, he made me sign a document that now included various details. Later they took me to another place, under heavy police guard. They shoved me into another dirty and depressing building. We went down four floors in a lift. When the doors opened I felt a chill as I saw prisoners dressed in the famous striped suit with their respective numbers. They took me into a room, removed my clothes and made me put on this same suit.

I guessed what the second act of this tragedy would be. The situation was now insufferable and I felt powerless. "Sir, I am not a terrorist. I'm innocent. Why are you doing this to me?"

"You will put it on or we'll hit you. You know how it goes!"

Full of anger and the feeling of powerlessness, I began to cry like a child. The younger policemen joked and laughed, "What problems will you have if you stay so pretty?"

Everything was decided. They took me out for the public presentation. The loudspeakers announced, "Now we present Juan Malléa, the author of the 'graves at Cieneguilla' paper!"

Two policemen in dark glasses took me before the journalists. My mind went blank. All I could see was a sea of cameras, with lights and flashes going off in my face. I lost the strength to react. I felt my dignity fall to the floor. While I was standing there all I could do was look; I couldn't speak a word. God gave me those moments of grace. Just like when he was on the cross, without screaming, without shouting.

The following day, upset and indignant, I thought of my family and of the other Christians who, like me, understood nothing and who perhaps now doubted my innocence. I thought a great deal about my father. About how he would feel at seeing this. He had been a policeman and had been awarded a medal of honour.

## II

After everything had been shown on television, my wife went back to DINCOTE in another attempt to secure my freedom. There she met German Vargas and Alfonso Wieland, Christians who introduced themselves as lawyers from the National Evangelical Council. They directed her to the institution. Before beginning, they wanted to make sure that I was innocent. The pastor of our church, Walter Agurto, had already submitted a document regarding my case. In addition, journalists from Channel 4 had been preparing a report to gain public support for my release.

The proof that they cited was a comparison of my handwriting with that of the famous "manuscript". Until now, however, it had not been examined by any serious or respected graphologist. Nevertheless, President Alberto Fujimori, while in Brazil, had announced that they had captured the Shining Path group that had executed the professor and the students at Cantuta University. In addition, when they had presented me to the press, they had also produced a typewritten paper signed by a Captain Urcias y Dominguez that read, "The original drafts of the 'manuscript' submitted to the provincial prosecutor's office and published by the magazine *Si*, come from the hand of Juan Abelardo Malléa. Although he disguised it, it is his handwriting." There was not a single periodical that didn't publish this statement.

At this point I was informed that CONEP had assigned a lawyer to work on my behalf. Earlier, the judge had ruled that the handwriting should be re-examined. It was very difficult to find a graphologist, because no one wanted to risk the anger of the state. In the end an expert, an officer named Guillermo Neyra Castro, accepted the job. After a detailed study of my handwriting he concluded that it did not match that on the manuscript.

Just so that there would not be any doubt left it was also sent to a North American expert in the USA. It was examined by an ex-FBI agent, who came to the same conclusion: the writing on the manuscript did not come from my hand.

In the meantime, my case had been presented before Congress as a human-rights violation. There, the president of the Commission on Human Rights, Congressman Roger Caceres Velasquez, together with Dr Gloria Helfer, took advantage of the presence of a number of graphology experts from all over the world who happened to be attending a conference in Peru. Their results matched the others.

Three months went by. I had the findings of three graphology experts in my favour. The provincial public prosecutor was forced to submit his opinion that there was no merit in the trial because they could find no evidence against me.

Regardless of this, however, the document number 529–93 was sent to the Special Court for Terrorism, where, outrageously, it was stalled for about six months.

As for me, I was transferred to the Castro Castro Prison on September 24th. We were in a group of about 300 men – they handcuffed us in pairs. Just as we had been told, we received kicks and beatings at the hands of the policemen. Guilty or innocent – we were all no more than prisoners in this jail. We were forced to remain inside freezing-cold cells for 23½ hours per day. When our half-hour outside arrived, we ran like freed animals in order to make up for lost time. That half-hour allowed us to enjoy the fresh air, to see daylight and, if we were lucky, to take advantage of any rays of sunlight that might allow us to warm ourselves a little. That moment of sunlight passed very quickly. Afterwards we would return to our cells, behind bars, as if we were dangerous beings.

As if to break our dignity down even more they passed our food to us through a little window right on the floor – it was the same place the rats went through at night. The food was badly made and tasteless. But it was all that we received each day, so we took advantage of it.

Visits took place only once a month and only immediate family members were allowed to come. It was a frustrating experience; there was a well-installed steel grille that separated us from our visitors. Everyone spoke at the same time for more than ten minutes, as all of our mutual pent-up emotion escaped. Or, perhaps, more accurately, we shouted and repeated ourselves in order to be heard. Because of the abrupt change from light to shadow it was impossible to distinguish the features of the visitors and when tears began to overflow the time was already short. We felt absolutely crushed not to be allowed even to touch hands – an embrace was impossible.

I remember that once my son, who was born during my

absence, was brought to me just ten days after his birth. He had to go through the entire security procedure in order to be allowed entry. He waited for hours in order to be allowed to enter with his mother. He was undressed; they took off his nappy and covered his little body with stamps. What had this little boy done wrong except have a father who was wrongly imprisoned? He couldn't enjoy my love for him, not a kiss or a cuddle, because prison security forbade it.

In prison I got to know people whose lives I could never have imagined. Some were innocent like me; others were not. In my cellblock there were many people who were ill with tuberculosis. Some of them coughed up blood, and others were already at an advanced stage of the illness. If they needed treatment they were given medicine, but the poor quality of the food in the prison didn't help anyone and it seemed as though their lives were being snuffed out. Another man had appendicitis but no one believed him when he said he felt ill. As a result he was on the verge of death when they finally evacuated him. Because he was considered a blemish on society, however, even at the hospital he was put on a non-urgent list and by the time they finally examined him it was too late. Later, we saw how because of the medical negligence his entire stomach had swelled up.

There were others who became psychologically unbalanced because of their imprisonment. Some of them went mad, or were on the verge of doing so and tried to commit suicide. AIDS also took its victims. One inmate who did not know he was HIV-positive lent his razor to another prisoner, who cut and infected himself. The people who suffered through these situations included those who were innocent – people who had been implicated by DINCOTE or by "faceless judges", for whom doubt was sufficient to condemn them.

Throughout my period of imprisonment, I also remember a

point when we were forced together with about 80 common prisoners. We went through four days like that, prevented from being able to sleep. At night we remained standing or sitting down. But God sent someone to share his food with me. During those days other prisoners would often come to my cell and ask, "So, you're the famous Juan Malléa, are you?"

"Yes, I'm Juan Malléa, but I'm not famous – I'm just here because of a mix-up," I would reply.

"How can you say you're not famous when all the journalists write about you and even the church is defending you! They say that you're innocent, and that the police made a mistake when they arrested you. What a big shot you are, man!"

At another point one of the Shining Path members approached me. "Hello! I'm Moises," he introduced himself.

"Moises? What a beautiful name! Your parents must have been Christians to give you such a biblical name."

"You're right," he said to me. "My parents are Christians. I was also a Christian, but I grew away from it because I saw that some of the other Christians were bad examples. They said one thing but lived another."

"But Moises, you should know that your commitment is to God alone and not to other people. I'll pray for you that you might return to the Lord's path."

"Thank you, brother," he answered me.

When we had the chance, when we weren't allowed to go out to the patio, we would organise ourselves to sing from our cells from Lamentations 3:25–36, which says that a man should quiet himself and review his life. He should feel remorse for his sins before crying out. Inside myself, I thought that as a sinner before God I could not cry out that I was innocent and unfairly treated. This was not an option. But before man's laws, I could definitely proclaim my innocence.

Christmas of 1993 arrived and I was still in the maximum-security prison. I was truly sad that under those circumstances I was unable to share this time with my wife and my children. On Christmas Eve, we asked to be allowed to leave our cells in order to offer up a prayer to the Son of God. I was very aware of the divine power of our Lord and, although I was still a prisoner, I knew that, through him, the truth would be exposed bit by bit by his light. It was just at that same time that investigators concluded that those who had executed the students in Cieneguilla were actually members of the "Colina Group".

One afternoon in April 1994 someone told me, "Malléa, you're going to be a free man."

I'd heard this many times before. I thought it was just another joke. But when the guard came to my cell with a paper in his hand I realised that it was true.

"Quickly, get your things together. Or would you rather stay here?"

My freedom was real – I had a hard time believing it! The free world had opened its doors wide to me. As they unlocked my cell, and as I walked out, I wanted to say goodbye and hug each one of those whom I was leaving behind, but I was not permitted to do so. They were all inside, under lock and key. I felt very sad about this. They registered me and checked the things I was taking with me. On the way out of the door I was accompanied by my father and by my lawyers, Dr José Regalado and Dr German Vargas. Then, at a distance, I made out my two children, my wife, and my brother. Those were unforgettable moments, full of happiness. I was able to embrace each one of them and to express my infinite affection for them. My eyes clouded with tears at being able to see them all again.

My time in prison had also caused damage in my family. My

little son, Juanito, whom I had left at nine months, was now over 1½ years old. He was used to being only with his mother and could not accept me.

"You're not my daddy. Go away!" he repeated over and over, as he cried.

He could not comprehend how someone could arrive in his life this way.

After fifteen days of freedom we were blessed with a trip to Pucallpa-Yarinacocha to stay for a month at the Summer Linguistic Institute. It was a wonderful time of retreat together with our children. We learned a great deal and returned home much more comfortable with one another.

After we returned, the brothers and sisters at Peace and Hope looked for a way to continue to reintegrate my family. They thought it might be necessary for us to go a bit farther away together. So we travelled again – this time all the way to Santiago, in Chile. There a group of psychologists met with us and gave us family therapy in order to diminish the effects of my imprisonment. Thanks to that, our son Juanito was later able to identify himself with me again.

## III

In December 1994 we returned to Lima to start again. There was a period when I did not want to leave the house. I had the idea in my head that when I got to the corner they would arrest me again. Thanks to God, I have now overcome that. But at times, together with my family, we sense that they continue to watch us, because we often see the same people in the different places we go to. I remember that, at the same time that I left prison, another man named Segundo Rojas Hernando also left. A few days after leaving the prison he met with a very strange death. It seemed that our innocence was not actually all that clear, to the point where we felt that the National Intelligence Service or even the Shining Path might want to take reprisals against us, because we had always spoken out publicly against their methods of violence.

After one year of freedom my car had still not been returned to me. When I went to claim it, they told me that DINCOTE had not given them any documents pertaining to my freedom. In their eyes, I was still a prisoner. Indignant, I asked for and was able to talk to the director. Thanks to God he was also a Christian, and we were able to talk together. He interceded on my behalf and ordered that my car be returned to me directly. However, when they took me to the car park I immediately spotted mine. It was totally destroyed and completely unusable. I knew that someone else had used it and had wrecked it. I had a tow truck take it back to my house and was forced to sell it for a much lower price than my family actually needed. They never returned my file or the personal documents that had been confiscated at my detention.

Later, when I went in search of a job I was asked for documentation on my police record and any stays in prison. I went to request them and was told that I was still officially on record as having been a terrorist. My name had still not been erased from the register. I had to go back to the Ministry of Justice with a lawyer in order to present a written request.

We lived through a period of extreme financial difficulty. I was worried about our son, but at the same time I trusted in the promise of the Lord, "It is not right that anyone should lack bread". Later this promise was fulfilled; the brothers and sisters from the organisation Open Doors gave us an offering that helped us a great deal. Thank God for them! Later, the blessing of the Lord fell on us again and I was able to buy a car in order to work with it and take care of my family.

Today the joy of my freedom has given me one overriding

desire: to do something for those innocents who remain in prison. I want to give something to those with no protection, who have been taken away from their homes in the provinces, who lack lawyers and family, who are alone. I remember that many of them would call me their countryman.

I particularly remember one, whom we called the "Piurano". He was Quechua-speaking and was illiterate. He despaired of ever being able to learn to read or write. "Juan, please find me a notebook; teach me the alphabet," he said to me. At times I would listen to him singing melodies in his own language, sad songs about loved ones who were far away. His moans and laments remain fixed in my mind. This has inspired me to return to the prison. I can see how the hand of God has opened a way for this.

One day I went along to the prison with the brothers from Peace and Hope. I had no documents, which meant there was no way I'd be allowed to enter, but they recognised me, and this was sufficient. Being back inside seemed incredible to me. One prisoner called out to me, "Malléa!"

I signalled to him to lower his voice. When I arrived at the cells I was overcome by a very strong emotion; I stretched out my hands to my friends. Some thought that I had been imprisoned again, but it was not true. I was there to fulfil the word of the Lord, "The Holy Spirit is with us and he has consecrated us to take the good news to the poor, to proclaim freedom to the prisoners, and to bring liberty to the oppressed".

Later, I requested my official identity card as Pastoral Agent for INPE (the National Penitentiary Institute). After going over a few hurdles I finally managed to obtain it. Now, thanks to God, I can visit my brothers and work with them on any occasion.

Just as when Peter was in prison, well looked after, our church prayed a great deal, and that, together with the calls from many institutions and the work of Father Hubert Lanssiers and the Ombudsman, was seen and heard by the Lord who answered. Pardons became a reality. Because the word "pardon" actually means pardon for a wrong committed, some refuse to accept it – but it was an opportunity that God gave many to enjoy freedom and the company of their loved ones.

On 1st October 1996 the first group of pardoned prisoners was released. We watched on television as a group of women came out of the Santa Mónica Prison. My attention focused on one old woman who had long, grey braids and wore a traditional skirt. My wife and I called her "the mami". With great emotion, she carried her things out of the door of the prison. I was interested in her and went to visit her. Her name was Liduvina, and later she became ill and was sent to hospital.

That same day we saw many others come out of the prison, including Pelagia Salcedo, who had spent four years in the Santa Mónica Prison. Her husband was also freed the same day. A little while later Saúl Tito Coicca left the prison, along with some others. We understood that the Lord was working and answering our prayers.

## Notes

1  While he was in prison a terrorist was brought to his cell. He had been shot and the wound was infected. He begged for a doctor but no one paid him any attention. Juan, moved by his plight, did the impossible and found help for the wounded man. Later he found out that the man was one of the terrorists responsible for the death of his friend. At that moment Juan remembered what he had asked God, but he no longer felt any hatred for the young man. He thought to himself, "This is a message from God."

2 Juan remembers this period between tears. Upon his release from prison, his children had only the same clothes they had bought that day. Those were the last clothes and the last toys they were able to buy. "The Lord was preparing me," he says.

# CHAPTER TWO

# SANTOSA

Santosa arrived in Lima when she was fourteen years old. In her native village of San Isidro de Ractay, in the Apurimac district of Grau province, Santosa had attended primary school. Her responsibilities of looking after the livestock and farming, however, left little time for her to complete her studies. In addition, in the highlands of Peru education is often perceived as more for boys than for girls. Many parents ask, "What is the point of girls studying?"

In Lima, Chela, as her friends called her, worked as a maid. In 1977 she was married, at the age of 21, and became a devoted housewife. That same year, her husband contracted a rare illness. Medical treatment failed to help and he lost weight and suffered from pain and blackouts. During this period, through the caring work of the "Light and Truth" Pentecostal Church of Peru he came to know Christ. The church was located near their home in El Planeta, near Argentina Avenue in Lima.

He was now an evangelical Christian but he was still ill. One night he woke up in tears and told Santosa about a dream he had had. God had drawn near to him, plunged his hands into his chest, and pulled out a toad. Then he washed him in crystal-clear water. The dream proved to be real! The illness, represented by the toad, left his body. "I'm healed! I'm healed!" he told Santosa. After that he stopped taking his medicine and soon afterwards was completely recovered.

Santosa witnessed the healing of her husband and knew that it was an act of God. This miracle led Santosa to faith, and from that point on both she and her husband were active members of their church.

Up until 1984 they had been renting their house in El Planeta. Rental costs had risen, however, and their family had grown with the birth of their third son, Saúl. This prompted them to look for a new place to live. Along with a number of other families they "invaded"[1] or squatted on a piece of land near the Duenas Bridge in the Lima district of San Martín de Porres. Problems arose when the police arrived and cordoned off the area, preventing anyone from leaving or entering. For those inside, with no food or water, this was torture. Santosa was on her own, enduring hunger and thirst while looking after their building materials of matting and poles.

In this predicament she prayed, "Lord, not my will, but yours be done." At the limits of her own strength, she fell asleep and had a dream. In the dream she saw two large irrigation canals brimming with water. There were plots of land ready for planting and a group of people parcelling them out on each side.

A man approached her. She could not see his face but simply heard him say, "This is not for you. Leave this place." He gave her a set of keys. She took them, opened a door, went up to the second floor of a house and then back down again. "This is your house. That is your key," said the man.

When the sun rose Santosa awoke. Her mind was made up and she abandoned their plot. Her husband had heard about land in Santa Martha, on the outskirts of Lima. There were no houses, no transportation, much less water and electricity – only stones and sand. Plots of land were for sale, however, and they decided to buy one. They invested nine years of savings in a plot they had never seen.

When they arrived at their new piece of land Santosa was amazed. It was exactly as she had dreamt. "God has given me this land," Santosa declared.

The next day she went to retrieve their matting and poles but decided to wait a few days before moving in. As she waited Santosa was puzzled to see a number of lorries in the Avenida Argentina, filled with building materials. She learned that the people who had sold them the land were traffickers in land who, in collusion with the mayor of San Juan de Lurigancho, were planning to take back the land, including Santa Martha, by force. They were planning to take advantage of the Christmas celebrations to do the deed. That night, however, everyone stayed in their shacks in order to protect their plots of land. After that they were left to live there in peace.

Their involvement with church became less intense after moving to Santa Martha. Eventually some of their fellow believers visited them and conducted prayer vigils in their home. Later, in 1987, a Pentecostal church, "Philadelphia", was founded in Santa Martha. Santosa, however, always felt most comfortable in their first faith community.

From the beginning Santosa regularly met with her neighbours to try to work together to improve the area. In 1984 they succeeded in setting up the "Glass of Milk" project, which the mayor of the city, Alfonso Barrantes Lingan, had initiated as part of his programme to combat poverty.

The "Glass of Milk" evolved to include other forms of nutrition and finally became a well-organised public canteen. Improving living standards, however, is not solely a matter of food. Santosa trained to promote health and nutrition, working with other institutions and giving talks. She worked with the "Flora Tristán" Institute, INPPARES (integrated reproductive health and business training) and others.

In those days the area lacked basic services such as roads and public transport. In 1989 Santosa, together with leaders from 37 different shanty towns around San Juan de Lurigancho, agreed to petition the municipality for official registration of their properties. A document to this effect was essential if they were to obtain water, sanitation and electricity.

All of their efforts to obtain this document proved fruitless. As a result, the same year, thousands of the inhabitants of the 37 shanty towns marched on the government's palace to demand registration of the municipality.

The police reaction was not slow in coming. Dust and sweat were soon mixed with truncheon blows and tear gas. 138 people were detained in DINCOTE for 24 hours. Santosa was among them. A few congressmen immediately called for their release.

In spite of the suffering it caused, the march was a success. The leaders immediately united themselves to organise payments for the installation of water, sanitation and electrical systems. This would also allow for the construction of roads and the introduction of public transport into the area. The whole process took several months. First the electricity was installed, and then, just one week before the completion of the water and sanitation systems, Santosa was detained by the police. Three days later, her husband abandoned their home and their children.

Santosa was deprived of her freedom until 24th February 1995, and was held in the Santa Mónica Prison in Chorrillos in Lima. Today she continues helping in the community canteen and also works with woollen garments and other types of clothing. Her children support her in everything but are limited because of the chronic unemployment in Peru. At times she feels that her home is a heavy burden without a partner with whom to share it.

Santosa writes here about her joys and anxieties during her stay in prison.

# I

It was 2:00 am on 26th February, 1994. I was awakened by the sound of the door being beaten down. I was frightened and thought it might be a drunkard. "Pepe, Pepe!" I whispered to my husband. We did not want to get out of bed for fear of waking the baby.

"Open up!" someone shouted from outside. "It's the police! Open up, terrorists! We've come to take you away."

I was slow to open the door as I had to look for my keys. In the meantime, several of the policemen had climbed up on to my neighbour's roof. The walls of our house were up but we did not have a roof yet.

I had barely got the door open when they all burst in, noisily and violently. There were six or seven of them. Immediately they began to go through our things. They accused me of giving food to terrorists and said I must be one too. I told them that they were mistaken.

At the time I was president of the public canteen run by the Santa Martha and San Juan de Lurigancho cooperative. Four or five girls worked with me and were a great help. I'd only recently given birth and was suffering from prolapse, so was not allowed to lift anything very heavy.

"The lady is ill and can't lift heavy objects or cook, but she can be here to supervise," the girls at the canteen had decided.

I recalled that TECNIOBRAS had recently been working in

our area, setting up water and sanitation. Many of the workers came to eat at the canteen. I thought that perhaps there had been an infiltrator among them, but then the police began to list women's names.

"Do you know this woman? You know who she is, don't you? Yes you do!" they continued.

"I don't know what her name is, but yes, it is true that she's come to the canteen to eat – not to my house but to the public canteen. She didn't force us to give her food. She came together with a tall, dark lady who brought her baby and a girl of eleven or twelve. They had asked for food, 'Señora, please could you give us some food, even if it's just a few scrapings of rice?'"

I explained to the police that I had not had any idea that she was a terrorist. Many people came asking for food, but it had nothing to do with terrorism. They were just genuinely needy people.

The police looked through everything, lifting up our mattresses and opening drawers. They went into the kitchen but found nothing. I told them I was a Christian and had nothing to hide.

"Oh, of course, we were told that you were a 'sister' – a 'sister terrorist', huh? We don't care if you're a Christian. Hurry up and get dressed. You're coming with us," they retorted.

"Where are you taking me? Let me take my baby," I asked, but they were not interested.

My husband only managed to say, "How can you take my wife away? And the baby . . . ?"

My baby was breast-fed and had never taken any other milk or solids. But they refused to let me take her with me.

"You'll be back tomorrow," said one of the policemen. But they did not release me. It was a year before I would return home.

The year that I was in prison the devil entered my home and my husband abandoned us. Although he was a believer and it was through him that I had come to faith, he ran off with another woman and never came back.

At 3:00 am, when they still had found nothing, the public prosecutor said, "Sign here."

The document said that they had not found anything. My husband and I both signed. They put me in a car and told me that there was a "repented terrorist" in the next car along and that he had accused me. I had never seen the man before but he knew my name. They took me to DINCOTE.

"Surely you know more – speak!" they persisted.

I learned later that the man's name was Almanso Lopez. They put the accused on one side and the "repented terrorists" on the other. I caught sight of him for one moment. He was a slim young man. I made out his features but I did not recognise him. I had never seen him before, not even in the canteen.

In DINCOTE they took me into a room and blindfolded me with a red cloth. They pushed me against the wall with my hands behind my back and said to me, "Stay standing there."

"Yes, I'll stay standing," I replied.

While all of this was happening I could hear men being beaten, and I thought of God and prayed to Jesus, "Just as you were innocent and went to the cross, so help me and help these men."

They did not come to beat me but I was left standing there all day and all night. While I was there they came and said to me, "Talk! If you confess and give us a name we'll let you go."

I did not know any terrorists, so what could I say? I was not going to lie and accuse an innocent person. "I don't know anything," I told them.

The next day was the same. They kept me like that for 48

hours. Then they took me to a tiny cell in which there was already another girl.

"Don't cry," she said to me.

She also was innocent and had been brought in because another "repented terrorist" had accused her. We comforted each other.

I was in DINCOTE for almost fifteen days. My relatives brought me breakfast and lunch but not dinner. The police let me have what they did not want but kept the best food for themselves.

I shared the gospel with the girl who was in my cell. I told her that God was good and that he would help us. I prayed and fasted.

While I was in DINCOTE, however, they took us and made us put on striped uniforms that looked like sacks. Sobbing, I turned to God, saying, "Why do you delay so long, until even the devil puts his clothes on me?"

A policeman heard what I said and responded, "I'm not the devil. I too believe in God."

"Yes, and Satan also believes in God," I told him.

He did not answer. They took us before the press and presented us as if we were terrorists: "We now present 'Comrade Vicky'!"

"Glory to God!" I exclaimed, because I believed in him.

I knew that neither the police nor the journalists had spoken the truth.

After this they took us by car back to DINCOTE. As I am a little overweight and my hands were tied, they had to help me in and out of the car.

Two days later they took us to the jail in the Palace of Justice. We stayed there for seven or eight days. There were prisoners who had been accused of common crimes there, and also those who were accused of terrorism. There was no toilet in any of the cells. We were taken out at 6:00 am and at night to go to the bathroom. Then we were returned to our cells. I did not know many people there, except for a woman who had been falsely accused. She had asked a labourer to watch her home. He had taken advantage of her absence, however, to steal all her belongings. When she had tried to retrieve her things, he had denounced her as a terrorist, and for this reason both she and her husband had been imprisoned.

In those days I used to always wear a black T-shirt and skirt, because my father had passed away. Some time later, on January 19th, my brother also died, in a road accident. His car had been struck by a rock during an avalanche. I had then been detained on February 26th. It seemed as if I were beset by misfortune. Faced with all this, I thought to myself, "A Christian always has to undergo trials, and if they don't go through them they are not approved by God." I remembered Job and Jonah. If Jonah was flung into the sea on account of his disobedience, and Job suffered leprosy and scabies even though he was loved by God, I ought to be able to put up with being in prison. I also remembered Paul and Barnabas: "Send me my cloak and the parchments, which are very important", and so I said, "Send me leaflets, and send me my Bible."

## II

I was transferred to Santa Mónica prison at night. I was assigned to cellblock C, cell 8, a punishment cell. In the end, however, they put me in an ordinary cell with other women and girls.

"When did you arrive? Where are you from?" they asked me.

"I am a Christian, an evangelical."

"But why have they brought you in here, then?"

"Precisely for that reason, because believers must face persecution too," I told them.

Although none of the three women with whom I shared the cell was a believer, they were all very good to me. They gave up the bed and covered me up with blankets. They were glad that I had joined them.

"We don't want you to cry. Are you hungry?"

"No, thank you. I can't eat."

I was fasting and I did not eat for three days. While in prison I fasted on various occasions, and just before I was freed I fasted for seven days. It had good results.

Later, thanks to the lawyer Pilar Aguilar from the Legal Defence Institute, I was moved to cellblock A where there was a group of Christian women, including Pelagia Salcedo. I had known Pilar Aguilar since the organisation "Flora Tristán" had sent her to see me two days after I was detained.

"Your case is very difficult; things are getting harder; we might not be able to intervene . . ."

"But, Doctor, I haven't committed any crime. I haven't done anything wrong . . ."

"But that's not what the authorities say. They're blind," she answered me. Then she then tried to reassure me. "Don't worry, they won't do anything to you."

On one occasion the commander came to see me. He asked me a few things and later brought me a whole pile of photos.

"Look at these – I want to see if you recognise anyone!"

I did not recognise anyone, except the little girl who was with the lady they had asked me about when I was detained. That was the only interview I was given. I never had a trial at Santa Mónica either. When I learned that I would be going before a "faceless judge" I asked God, "Why do I have to go before a 'faceless judge', Lord, if your judgement is coming soon and I want to be present there?"

I remember that there was a man in the prison who was in charge of carrying documents. He told me, "Señora, they're keeping you here just because they want to. It's better to be an ambassador from I don't know where. Letters arrive for you every day from all over the world. Your brothers and sisters have not forgotten about you."

Dr Aguilar had recommended that I write back to them, telling them how I felt. I sent a letter to Holland: "I was in prison and you visited me, naked and you clothed me". I wrote various Bible passages and then mail started to arrive, including some from Canada.

While I was in prison I remember meeting a Catholic woman who was very much a believer. "Are you an evangelical?" she asked me.

"Yes, I am an evangelical."

"I'm a Catholic and I believe firmly in God."

We sang together, "Leave the stone and let the water flow . . ."

One day a lady, seeing me cry, said, "Don't cry. You'll end your life that way, and you need to stay alive for your children. If you have a daughter, think of her. Where are you from?"

"I'm from Apurimac, in Culpahuasi district in Grau province. I'm from the Layme Bejar family."

"I'm a Contreras, Jesusa Contreras. Do you know Inocencio Contreras? He's my brother."

"Yes, I know your brother. He has a lot of cattle."

Jesusa, my fellow countrywoman, and I shared meals together and kept each other company.

Psalm 51 was a great help to me during my imprisonment: "Have mercy on me, O God, according to thy steadfast love; according to thy abundant mercy blot out my transgressions." Before that, I had read the Bible but had perhaps not understood very much. But I loved God, and in prison I learnt more. I learnt to read and to write better. "Lord, speak to me now, teach me and prepare me," I asked him.

On one occasion I fasted in the hope that the judges would be just for once, as God commands. Although I longed to be free, I was able to calm my desperation by remembering Paul and Barnabas, who were in prison and stayed inside even after an earthquake; after that they were freed.

I was assigned to kitchen work while I was in prison. One day the colonel asked if I would help out in the kitchen, and I agreed. As I was unable to lift things the young girls helped me. They lifted the pots and I served the food. This work helped me a lot, lifting my spirits and giving me a breath of freedom.

During my imprisonment I was visited by my brother and my oldest son, who is now in Chile. My husband did not come. My children were left virtually abandoned in the house. Only my younger sister stayed with them, and my oldest son, who had arrived from the mountains, went to work on a building site in order to provide food for them.

Every night in prison, the guards used to take a woman who could read cards out of her cell. They didn't take us, because we were Christians. But God has his plans and by his will all things are done. I recall that one night someone woke me up as I was sleeping.

"Sister, sister, can you wake up? I want you to pray for us." It was one of the guards.

When I went along the passage and we went down to the patio, I saw that all the guards from cellblocks A, B and C had gathered together. There were about 18 of them.

"Lord, you speak for me," I said.

As I began to speak they all got down on their knees.

"In the power of Jesus Christ! The blood of Jesus has

power! There is power in the Lord!" I reprimanded them, forcefully. "May they understand your word! I want them to believe in you, Lord. Show them that you exist. You are the Almighty God," I prayed and prayed aloud with all my strength.

Suddenly it wasn't me speaking; it was a demon, saying, "We don't want to come out. We're staying here!"

And Jesus, with a voice like thunder, speaking through me, exclaimed: "I am Jesus Christ! Get out of this jail! I reproach you, enemy! You cannot stand against me!" The voice was so loud that I felt sure that all Chorrillos and all of Lima could hear it.

Then, near me, I heard a policewoman called Gladys saying, "Lord, I recognise that I am disobedient, but now I am going to do your will. Watch over me, Father."

Further away, another young woman, Rocío, burst into tears. She sobbed like a little girl, and cried out, "Glory to God!"

Several were converted that night – I later saw in their work that they really did belong to the Lord. Everything finished at about 1:00 am.

The next day there was some talk among the inmates who had heard the commotion, and they complained to the colonel, who called me in. When he asked, I truthfully told him all that had happened. I said that the guards had come looking for me, and that we had all prayed together.

"Oh dear! You've really gone too far this time!"

"The things of God belong to God," I explained. "This is all the Lord's will."

"It's alright, Señora. Just go," he said.

# III

My lawyers, Pilar Aguilar and Eduardo Vega, had requested a meeting with the "reformed terrorist" who had originally accused me. This had been refused by his own lawyer on previous occasions. He would not face up to what he had done, and the matter remained unresolved. When a "confrontation" was finally arranged, however, I remember the public prosecutor saying to me, "Tell the truth! Say that you know this man. Why don't you admit that you know him?"

"You'd be asking me to tell a lie. I don't know him, and I'm not here to condemn my fellow man. Judas did it, but I don't intend to."

Then the man, lowering his head, began to cry.

They asked him: "Do you know this woman?"

"Yes."

"Where have you seen her?"

"In her home."

"What was she doing?"

"She went into her house, and after that I don't know."

"What does her house look like?"

"With a roof. It's a completed building."

My house did not have a roof; it did not even have a floor. It was made of matting. He also said that I had big benches, which was not true.

The prosecutor went to my house, interviewed my young son and established that the man had lied. After the confrontation, they did not have anything. Since there was no proof, there was no case. They had found nothing with which to accuse me.

One day, only a short time after this happened, a man came to announce that I could go free. "Señora, you are a free woman. If I open the door, you are free to leave."

Since he was known for being a real joker, I told him that he was a liar and not to interrupt me, as I was singing with some of the other Christian women.

We continued to sing, but later a policeman appeared and said: "Señora Layme, they're calling you."

When I went down the passage, I made out Dr Vega, who said to me, "Señora, are we going or not? It's been a while now since we came to tell you what happened, and you haven't responded."

I realised that my freedom had finally arrived. My sisters, upon hearing the news, began to sing, "Free!"

The Christians who were left inside said to me: "Sister, when you leave, seek out the other Christians, speak to them and tell them that we're innocent. Shout to the four winds that we are not going to die. We will have eternal life. Don't be afraid, and keep praying. . . ."

That was how I got in touch with the brothers at Paz y Esperanza (Peace and Hope), to whom I told everything that was happening in the prison. True, at that time it was very hard for religious workers to enter the prisons, but God would open the doors.

When I left prison a friend, Lucho, from "Flora Tristán", was waiting for me. He had visited my children regularly throughout my imprisonment – in fact my baby came to call him "Daddy". He was always sending me little notes, and other things. He became like a son to me.

Lucho was in the doorway. When we saw each other, he smiled with tears in his eyes. He stepped forward, embraced me, and wept for joy. We climbed into a car and went to the Legal Defence Institute (IDL). A lot of photos were taken of me there, and we spoke with a great many people. They sent faxes to the international press, and especially to Amnesty International.

We went to "Flora Tristán". It was 7:00 pm, but no one had moved. Everyone was still waiting for me in the reception room. When I arrived they began to ask me how I was. They all cried, and I did too. Then they started asking questions, "Where did you come from?"

"From Paris. I had a stopover in Canada and now I'm in Peru."

Everyone laughed and said that I hadn't changed. They were very happy. We had a toast, and I told them that I wasn't going to drink liquor, so they gave me a soft drink. We enjoyed pleasant conversation, and later Diana Miloslavich, Inga and Lucho took me home. They bought roast chicken and soft drinks for my children. Lucho got out of the car and knocked on the door.

"Mr Lucho, what are you doing here at 11:00 pm?" asked my son.

I was in the car and couldn't bear it any longer. I got out quickly and entered the house. My children were watching TV, and my little daughter, who was lying down, complained that her chest was hurting. She asked to be suckled, and began to nurse. For God, one day is a year, and a year is a day. For God, nothing is impossible.

My friends left at about 1:00 am. I couldn't stand any more, and sent my son to find a friend of mine, a Jehovah's Witness named Maria Zapata. That night I stayed sitting up until dawn. I could not sleep. Everything had changed. My mattress was in shreds, my kitchen filthy, my house a disaster. When the clock struck five in the morning, I set to work washing and scrubbing everything from one end of the house to the other. I made breakfast for the children. When they got up, they began to work with me. My oldest son went off to work, telling me that he was about to be paid, it being Saturday.

I well remember meeting Celedonia Quispe. She cried as she hugged her baby to her chest. She too had been falsely accused of being a terrorist. When I saw her I began to weep and became her friend.

A few days after I met her, Celedonia was moved to my cell-block, and we were able to get to know each other more. As I dished out the food, I would secretly give her a larger portion, since she was breastfeeding her baby. She had suffered a great deal. She had been abandoned by her husband, who had taken their son, Roberto, aged three, and had left behind the two daughters, Juanita, eleven, and Haydee, who had just turned one.

Juanita took on the job of looking after Haydee. Every three months she carried the little one to the prison to visit their mother. They survived by selling jelly in the market at La Parada. While Celedonia was in prison, Juanita took charge of running the house, which meant that she was unable to attend school.

The day of my release, Celedonia asked me if I would look after her children.

"Do you know La Parada?" she asked.

"Of course I do."

"Enter by this street, then you will come to a women's bath house. They sell skin treatments there. Ask anyone for my children. They know me, because I used to go with my bucket and sell there too."

I promised her that I would find them and take them into my own home, and that is what I did. I did not have a job, so I knew it would be difficult, particularly as I already had a number of children to care for. But God was with me, and the children were in my charge for two years until Celedonia was freed.

Today, together with my children and with God's help, we

try to keep going. My husband is no longer at my side, but then, I do have a great family of fellow Christians, and loyal friends in the public canteen that I run. I am always meeting with other brothers and sisters who, like me, suffered unjust imprisonment. I give thanks to God because he has always been at my side.

## Note

1   "Invasions" were carried out because of the scarcity of housing in Lima. This consisted of organised, mass occupations of outlying, uncultivated land; the parcelling-out of lots, and a subsequent struggle for legal recognition of a new suburb.

# CHAPTER THREE

# AMBROSIO

Ambrosio first experienced abandonment before he was even born, when, in March 1972, his father abandoned the family. When Ambrosio was only two years old his mother died. He then moved through the homes of various relatives – starting in his birthplace, Ccollay in the province of Tayambamba, and then moving on to Chaquicocha, where he lived with his great-uncle, a member of the Christian and Missionary Alliance Church. He stayed there until he was twelve years old.

While in Chaquicocha he worked in the fields and with live-stock – alternating this with his work as a *criado*.[1] His guardians did not permit him to finish his primary studies and he lived in total dependence on his relatives. Ambrosio's entire life alternated between church and the fields.

Ambrosio was a dedicated member of the church youth group, and as such he had a very profound experience of church. He was very quick to understand the Bible lessons and the doctrinal teaching he received. He frequently took part in special presentations during the church services. Singing was his particular favourite.

The friendships he forged with other youths of his own age

widened his horizons. They motivated him to improve his condition in life. His friends had shoes; he did not. They had money with which to buy clothing; Ambrosio did not. Their parents supported their studies – Ambrosio had been unable to finish primary school. He had never had anything of his own; his clothes had always been hand-me-downs.

In 1985, before he had even turned thirteen years old, and although he felt at home at his church, he decided to travel to Tocache to work. Almost all of his friends had done the same thing. Ambrosio joined up with his cousin and together they set off in search of new horizons. The new distance between him and his relatives, however, also meant distance between him and his church.

In Tocache he dedicated himself to agricultural work. He received less pay than the adults but it was enough to cover his basic needs. He worked with a variety of different crops, including rice, corn, coca and others. At times the coca fields were raided by the police, which always caused general panic. However, because of his short stature and his youth, Ambrosio never had any problems.

He worked alongside his cousin and until they each went their separate ways he shared a hut with him as well. Ambrosio began to save his money and also purchased clothing and other basic items that he had never had before.

After one and a half years he was able to pay a visit to his relatives in Chaquicocha. When he returned to Tocache, Ambrosio went back to his agricultural work. He had friends who were employed in various lines of work, among them conducting the ferries that transported passengers from one side of the river to the other. Ambrosio learned how to drive the boats, and from 1990 to 1992 he worked as a ferryman in Tocache and Tarapoto. Halfway through 1992 he travelled to Aguaytia, where he continued in the same line of work.

The towns of Tocache, Tarapoto and Aguaytia, where most of Ambrosio's life was spent, are all located in San Martín department, in the forested region of Peru. The jungle and the swamps in this region make travel by land very difficult. As a result, travel by river is the best mode of transport. This method is used by all the inhabitants of the region, the businessmen and the merchants, but it also includes those people who have chosen to take up arms in Peru.

The poverty of the Peruvian jungle towns has led to the cultivation of coca as the principle economic activity in this region. This was an area that until a few years ago was a major supplier in international narco-trafficking.[2] The inaccessibility of the forests meant that it was easy to construct small airfields where the drug traffickers' small planes could land. This illicit activity, which involved millions of dollars, needed armed security, and the subversive groups provided it. In return they received large sums of money to carry on their armed struggle.

For this reason a large number of terrorists concentrated their activities in the jungle. Narco-trafficking became their principle source of income. This type of cooperation became known as "narco-terrorism", which later allowed the authorities to try many drug traffickers in military courts as if they were terrorists themselves.

It was under these circumstances that on 5th February 1993 Ambrosio was detained for transporting, unbeknown to him, members of a Shining Path rebel column.

After his imprisonment, Ambrosio was freed on 18th May 1995. He had been kept for six months in Aguaytia Prison, one year in the prison in Pucallpa, and four months in the prison in Huancayo.

He has now completed his secondary studies in night school and plans to study for a professional degree. Ambrosio gives the following testimony about his time behind bars.

# I

I was born in Tayabamba, a town located in the department of La Libertad. When I was two years old I lost my mother. I had never known my father, as he abandoned us when I was still in my mother's womb. I lived with some aunts and uncles until I was twelve years old and then I became independent. I left my village and went to live in Tocache. There I worked with coffee and cacao. My goal was to work in order to finance my college studies.

Later I went to live in Aguaytia. I worked as a motorboat conductor, transporting people each day. It was there that, on 5th February 1992, I was detained by the police.

I remember that that day, after leaving work, I arrived at my home at almost 11:00 pm. As I was extremely tired I went straight to my bedroom. Just as I was about to lie down I was surprised by the sudden entrance of a group of people.

"Is there anybody here?" asked one of them.

"Yes, what's happening? Who are you?" I asked.

I immediately got up and went to see who it was. When I saw that they were all in police uniforms and carrying all kinds of weapons, I was frightened. "What are you looking for, Señores?"

"Get down on the floor and don't raise your head!" they spat out.

As they abused me one of them pulled my hands behind my back and tied me up with a thick cord. Later they blindfolded me and shoved me out into a car. They kept me blindfolded as they drove to the police station. While they drove me I heard others saying, "It's him!"

When we arrived at the police station, they took me out onto the patio and began to interrogate me. "You're Comrade Dominguez, aren't you?"

"I'm *Ambrosio* Dominguez, not 'Comrade Dominguez'," I answered.

"Right, tell us everything you know," one of them said.

Three hours went by and I began to wonder why all of this was happening to me. I could not understand any of it, because I had never had anything to do with terrorists.

"Tell us about your comrades, little man; where are they?"

"I don't know anything, Señores. I'm not a terrorist."

"Listen, terrorist, do you think we're just messing around? You're not going to get another chance; you have to tell us the whole truth."

"I already told you, I don't know anything," I said.

"Alright, if you don't want to tell us willingly, we'll see if *now* you'll tell us!"

At that moment two policemen came up to me, lifted me and hung me up like an animal. They beat me and hung on my body. It was very painful. At certain moments I felt as though I would die. I cried out loudly. Finally they untied me, threw me to the floor and poured water over me.

Later they brought in a boy, a member of the Shining Path, and asked him, "Do you know him?"

"Yes, sir, I know him."

"He's a member of the Shining Path, isn't he? Yes or no?!"

"Well, I've never actually seen him with the group."

"But you said he collaborated with you, didn't you?!"

"Well, he's ferried us in his boat a few times."

"That's all we need! What are we waiting for?"

Right then I interrupted and said, "Sir, is this what you're accusing me of? I never interrogate the people I transport in my boat – that's not part of my job."

"You're the boat conductor?" the captain asked me.

"Yes, I have a boat."

"What do you do?"

"I take passengers from one side of the river to the other."

At that moment another policeman interrupted and said, "Hey, little man, do you think we're stupid enough to believe that you don't have anything to do with this? Do you steer with your eyes closed, or what?"

"I just do my work, and that's all. I don't get involved in my passengers' lives."

They started to beat me again. They rubbed electric wires against my hands. This almost killed me. I was unconscious for a few minutes. As I lay there in a semi-conscious state they continued to beat and kick me.

As they beat me they said, "You and all the other terrorists are going to wind up in prison. You'll be sentenced to at least 40 years if they don't give you life in prison! That's the destiny of dogs like you."

This scene was repeated over and over for fifteen days. Kicks, slaps, electricity . . . at night I could not sleep because my whole body hurt so badly. There was no bed and the floor was always very damp. In addition, I had to share a cell with the man who had implicated me. It was very difficult being so close to him, because I felt a great deal of anger about what had happened.

"I never thought you could do this to me," I said to him.

"But it was only because they tortured me and forced me to accuse somebody," he defended himself.

"Fine! Maybe you collaborated, I don't care, but why did you have to involve *me* like this?" I insisted.

Four days later they transferred me to the marine base. Once there the torture and interrogations started all over again. They kept me in a pit of water for two nights in a row. One of those nights it rained torrentially but I was forced to stay there like that, with no protection. At daybreak I could no longer cope, and I began to cry bitterly. At that moment a policeman appeared. "I can't do anything to help you right now. I can only tell you one thing, you have to trust in God. He will give you strength." Later he brought me a cup of hot coffee.

"Thank you, officer."

"Don't thank me; give your thanks to God."

At 6:00 am they took me out of the well and took me into the showers. There, when I was totally naked, they began to insult me and beat me with a plank of wood. "You are a terrorist dog!"

"Please just kill me all at once: I can't stand any more beatings. You're not going to get anything out of me because I don't know anything," I cried out.

Later they put me in the showers to wash me off, but what they were really doing was trying to wash away the marks from the torture.

After this they took me to my cell. When they left me there, and as I rested, I began to think about the Lord and my relationship with him. I told him, "Lord, this is the moment to reconcile myself with you. I am an orphan; you know that; I have no mother. My father abandoned me and I have relatives who don't care about me. But I have you, and I realise that I have distanced myself from your presence. Right now I want to return to you."

The next day we were visited by a woman, who handed us some apples through the bars. Later she began to speak about God. "If there is anyone here who is a Christian but for any reason has grown away from God, I'm here to tell you that Jesus is ready to forgive you."

At that moment, those words were stronger than all the torture I'd received. I told myself, "I am that person; this is what I'm looking for." Later I went over to the bathroom, my soul overcome by sadness. I went back to my cell, where some of the others, noticing the state I was in, said, "Hey, what's wrong with you?"

I didn't reply but just meditated on what that woman had said. I could not take it any more, so I turned to God and said, "Lord, I'm seeking you now, and from this point I know that you are good, I know that there must be some reason why I am here. In reality, spiritually speaking I'm not innocent, I'm a sinner; but now I'll seek you."

After that point my life changed. I was freed from all my bitterness towards those who had unjustly accused me and even those who had tortured me. That same day, someone asked me, "When you get out of here, what are you going to do to get back at the people who did this to you?"

"I'm not holding it against anyone," I replied. "Only God can judge, and he will see that justice is done. I'm just going to try to live decently."

"Since when have you changed? You were always ready to get revenge on everyone who did this to you."

"Do you remember that woman who brought us the apples?" I asked him. "God used her, and through her I heard his voice. He freed me from all my bitterness and came back to forgive me for my errors."

The small prison in Aguaytia didn't receive any support from the state – the only way to combat hunger was to hope that those prisoners who had family nearby would share a little of their food with us. I stayed in that prison for six months, which were very traumatic because of the hunger and torture I had to go through.

Until that point I had never had a lawyer to defend me. So, alone and without any legal support, I went before a judge, who began his interrogation, "For whom were you transporting those boxes of beer?"

"I don't know anything about that; I took them to the dock. I don't know where they took them after that."

"You helped them take the boxes of beer to the house, didn't you?" he insisted.

"No, I carried on working."

"What religion do you belong to?"

"I'm an evangelical."

"Let's see, then, do you know any psalms?"

"Psalm 23: 'The Lord is my shepherd, I shall not want, he makes me lie down in green pastures' . . ."

"Hey, boy, the problem is that a lot of the Shining Path members know you and say that you are a collaborator," he replied.

After a few weeks I went back before the judge. Then they tried me and sentenced me. A month later I was transferred to Pucallpa.

## II

When I arrived at the San Pedro de Pucallpa Prison I met a captain whom I had known in Aguaytia. He had been in charge of visual inspections. At one point when I was there he had said to me, "You don't have anything to do with this terrorism business; perhaps you'll get out next week." He was very surprised to see me at Pucallpa, and came over to greet me. "Dominguez! What are you doing here?"

"They transferred me to this prison, Captain. My situation is still difficult but now I'm more peaceful. God has given me peace and now I've put my trust in his justice," I told him.

"Well, don't worry. I'll try to help you any way I can."

"Thank you very much. God will repay you."

"To start with, I'll put you in a less dangerous cell," he promised.

When he took me to the cellblock he said, "Listen, every-body. This boy is innocent; he doesn't have any parents and I'm going to ask you to treat him well."

After a few hours I realised that many of the men in that cellblock were people that I already knew.

"Dominguez! What are you doing here?"

"It's a long story; we'll talk about it later," I told them.

"But brother, you're a good man. What happened?"

"Don't worry, we'll help you out around here," another said to me.

A few days later I met a group of Christians who gathered together to praise the Lord. On the first day, one of them came over to me. "Hello! Are you a believer?"

"Yes, I am, brother," I said.

"Can you share your testimony with me?"

"Well, I became a Christian when I was young. I drifted away from the Lord but just a little while ago I was reconciled with him in the prison in Aguaytia."

We met once a week to share the Word. It was also a way to escape some of the negative thoughts that some of the other prisoners there tried to fill our heads with. We would sing choruses and many Christian brothers visited us to preach the Word. We also prayed a good deal. The group grew. Many men were converted and we grew to about 30 brothers. We all helped one another out, as much in the material as in the spiritual sense.

I remember the case of a mother whose son had been accused of rape. The old woman was at least 80 years old. I was deeply touched by seeing her, looking at her son through the bars, asking the policemen to allow her to hug and touch her son. A memory of my own mother came to my mind and I thought, "My God, I believe that if she were near she would do the same as that old woman."

There was one occasion when, while queuing for my food ration, I fainted. I was unconscious for about five minutes and my face changed colour. The other inmates told me this. When I regained consciousness I recalled how more than once I had thought to myself, "It would have been better for me to die than to go on suffering behind bars."

But being part of a group helped a good deal, and we fantasised about being reborn and having a happy childhood. We spoke face to face amongst ourselves. We came to our own conclusions, saying that prison did not rehabilitate but was rather a kind of torment, a long-drawn-out death. Others asked me what I would do when I regained my freedom. I told them that I would praise God and would finish my studies, which I had abandoned because of a lack of guidance and support.

There were people who smoked marijuana inside the prison, and they often offered to share food with me that their families had brought them, but I tried to stay away from them. Thankfully God gave me support through other people. I had a friend with whom I used to walk around the small courtyard. He was a great support because his family visited him every eight days. It seemed like a dream to me that strangers would become my friends, who in one way or another always lifted my spirits.

Once, one of these companions of mine fought with another inmate and was sent to the "can", or punishment cell. Because we were friends, I missed him. On the fourth day he was let out, but he told me that at any moment I was going to be transferred to Yanamayo, Huancayo or Trujillo Prison. I thought that a transfer would mean I was going to lose many of my friends, whom perhaps I would never see again. It made me very sad to think that I could lose my friends under these circumstances, and I remembered how Jesus cried when he lost his friend Lazarus. Whenever I heard about a possible transfer, I thought about it and said, "Lord, do your will; wherever they take me, you will be with me."

This is how the days went by. Each morning, I awoke hoping that my freedom would arrive soon. On 18th December at 8:00 am they took us out onto the patio. The captain approached us. "The moment of the transfer is here!"

The captain began to call out the names of those who would be transferred. About 45 of us were to leave. I ran back to my cell to get my things and everyone from my cellblock surrounded me.

"Dominguez, I want to give you my blanket so that you sleep covered up," a friend, named Marino, said.

"Here, take this money that all your friends from the cellblock have collected for you," said another.

These gestures touched me deeply, for I never expected such solidarity. Between tears and smiles I said goodbye to each one of them. Immediately I was directed to a bus that was waiting outside to take us to the airport.

As we travelled the policemen insulted us at every opportunity. "You are all dogs and that's why you have to die. Terrorists like you are a blemish on society. You don't deserve to live."

This angered me. Although a number of the prisoners were actually innocent they still treated us as if we were animals. I just said to the Lord, "Father, please take care of me. I don't know where we're going or what awaits us there; I just want to commit myself into your hands."

## III

When we arrived at Huancayo Prison, we were greeted with maltreatment and insults. Then one of the policemen came straight over to me. "And you? Where are you from?"

"I was born in La Libertad Department."

"Wow, boy – we're fellow countrymen! I'm also from Trujillo."

The major came over to us and asked him, "Do you know this boy?"

"Yes, Major, he's from the same place as me."

Later, the same policeman said, "Everyone from the coast and everyone from the north get over to one side. You'll be going to Cellblock C."

It was precisely that cellblock that was the least dangerous.

The next morning, the same captain came to my cell. "Boy, I've brought you a little food here. I know what it's like to be alone and not to have any family nearby."

"Thank you, sir; the truth is I don't know *how* to thank you. You've been very kind to me."

"Don't worry. I know that you are innocent."

Right then I got down on my knees and thanked the Lord, because I knew that this was his doing. It was his hand protecting me and sustaining me. Later, when I returned to the cellblock, I asked if anyone there was an evangelical, and somebody shouted, "I'm a Christian!"

"What's your name?" I asked him.

"Toribio Garrido," he answered me.

"God bless you, brother. We share the same faith. Do you know any other brothers here?"

"Yes, there are a few of us. We meet once a week to praise the Lord and also to read his Word. Sometimes we get together to fast and pray."

That day I joined the group of brothers and we began to preach the Word and pray constantly. I remember that one day we got together with Garrido and decided to dedicate the whole day to fasting and reading the Word of God. That day Toribio told me his testimony. "Look, brother, I want to be very honest with you. The truth is, I was part of the Shining Path. But the Lord freed me and took me away from all of that. Now I want to preach and practise peace, not violence."

He began to cry inconsolably and I hugged him. We cried together as I tried to comfort him. "I am very thankful for your honesty. I can only say that, if you *have* decided to put your hand to the plough, don't look backwards, and continue to enjoy the Lord's blessing. When God forgives us he forgets all the wrong we have done, because he loves us."

"Thank you, brother Ambrosio. How wonderful it is to have a brother at one's side and to hear the Word of God through one of his sons."

Fifteen days after I arrived at the prison in Huancayo we received a visit from the lawyers from the National Evangelical Council of Peru (CONEP). At about 4:00 pm a brother named Gaspar said to me, "Brother Ambrosio, they are Christian lawyers. Why don't you go over and tell them about your case?"

"I don't know; I don't think they can help me. They don't know me and they might not believe me."

"But try! The Lord could use this opportunity," Gaspar insisted.

His words motivated me, and I went over to one of them. It was Dr José Vinces. "Good afternoon, Doctor."

"Hello! What's your name?"

"Ambrosio Dominguez. I want to tell you about my situation and see if you can help me. I am a Christian and I'm innocent, but I don't have a lawyer."

"Don't worry; we'll study your case and consider it."

After this they said goodbye to us, but they returned the following week. This time Dr Vinces came with Dr Ruth Alvarado. After a few minutes, sister Ruth called me over. "How are you, Ambrosio?"

"A little worried, but I trust in the Lord."

"Good. Brother, we've studied your case and we can see that an injustice has been committed against you. We want to inform you that from this point on the Evangelical Council will take charge of your case. We have been appointed to assume your legal defence."

"Thank you, Doctor! May God bless you!"

After that, a few months went by. Then one morning Dr Vinces came to speak to me. "Brother Ambrosio, get ready, because tomorrow we're going to have your hearing."

"And what should I do, Doctor?"

"Just stay calm and trust in the Lord. I want to tell you that the brothers and sisters from many different churches and from many different countries are praying for you. Everyone at the Council is interceding for you in the hope that you will soon be released from prison."

I was left speechless. I was very surprised, because I could not imagine that so many people could be praying for me. When the hour arrived I left my cell and Dr Vinces accompanied me to where the judges were. One of them said, "Have you repented of what you did?"

"I can only repent before the Lord. But to repent of a crime that I did not commit? This I cannot do, because I am not a terrorist."

Later Dr Vinces intervened and began my defence – supporting my innocence. The judges listened attentively to him and later suspended the hearing until the 26th of the same month.

On the morning of the 26th, we re-entered the Audience Hall. The same judges were there. The strange thing was that they did not ask me a single question. After a few minutes of silence one of them announced that, after finding no irrefutable proof against me, they were declaring me INNOCENT.

# IV

When I left prison I asked myself what kind of attitude society would have towards me. What kind of reaction would people have towards someone who had been wrongly accused of terrorism? Would conversation be the same? Would they still offer me the same trust and friendship? Or would it be completely different? Would I be marginalised, rejected – would they keep their distance?

Once I was free, and before travelling to Lima, I was interviewed by Christians from Radio Maranatha in the city of Huancayo. For the first time I was given access to a means of communication. They supported me and stood by me. The next day I travelled to Lima at the invitation of the lawyers who were working at that time at CONEP. When they realised that I did not know anyone in Lima they sympathised with my situation and took care of me. As Jesus Christ said, "I had nowhere to lay my head", but they gave me help to cover my basic needs. After a few days I was able to locate a cousin, who received me in his humble home. He showed me trust and courage in those very difficult moments of my life. I give thanks to God for all of this. And, following his Word, I can say that I am certain that he chose me from my mother's womb.

The brothers at the Council lent me 440 New Soles (about £130) so I could start up a small business that would allow me to make the necessary income to support myself. But the testing did not take long to start again. The following day, as I went out to buy some clothes that I had planned to sell in Aguaytia, I was robbed of all my money. I was very angry with myself. I went to a park to think. It was a harsh blow. That day I cried as I have only rarely cried in all my life.

After giving vent to all my feelings I decided to go back to my cousin's house. He wasn't there but I met his wife, who upon seeing my face asked, "What happened to you?"

I opened my mouth but I could only say, "I was robbed."

"What are you going to do?" she asked.

"I don't know," I answered.

That afternoon I went to an evangelical church. Desperately, I searched for the pastor. When I found him I told him everything that had happened to me and asked if he could find me a job so I could pay back the money.

He told me, "Unfortunately, I'm sorry to have to say that I can't do anything to help you."

I felt disillusioned. After talking to the pastor I stayed for the service. There was a moment when we were meant to pray in pairs for each other's needs, but since I did not know anyone I stayed by myself. A brother came over to me, however, and asked me what needs I had. I answered that I had a lot of problems – above all a debt to the brothers at the Council, who although they hardly knew me had lent me money. This was the thing that bothered me the most – I thought that they might not believe my story about the robbery.

Upon finding no solution to my problem, I decided to tell them the truth. First I met with the social worker from Peace and Hope at CONEP and, after I had told her the whole story, she said, "What are you going to do? You've only just got out of prison and you don't have work. Let me talk to the director."

They talked for about 20 minutes but to me it seemed like an eternity. I asked myself, "Will they believe me? I'm sure that they're going to want me to give back all the money." I could not see any other way out.

Soon the social worker came back and explained to me what decision they had made. They had decided that in exchange for the money they had lent me I should work for a few weeks at CONEP. I thanked God and the brothers and sisters for their understanding. After feeling so deceived and sad, my hope and faith in God was reborn and strengthened.

Throughout the period that I worked at CONEP I got to know all the different people who worked there, and I began to forge a marvellous friendship with them. Once I had worked all the necessary days I began to wonder, "What is going to happen to me next? Where will I work?"

A desire rose up in me to continue working with the Council, and not for wages but just for my travel expenses. My request was accepted and from that point on my relationship with the Council has deepened and my friendship with the other workers has continued to grow.

While I was involved with the institute, the Christians at CONEP suggested that I should finish my secondary studies. They talked to me about it, told me about a private college and promised to cover all the costs. Once we had obtained the necessary information the brothers and sisters at Peace and Hope told me that each one of them was personally going to contribute money each month to cover my expenses. This good news moved me deeply. I could not believe it, but then I understood that God was working in my life according to his plan. The brothers supported me until January 1996, when, unfortunately, administrative problems led to the involuntary departure of a number of my coworkers. These events left me confused to the point at which I thought everything was going to fall apart, but I refused to give up, and although I did not understand very much about what was happening my faith in the Lord remained intact, and as I leaned on him I continued my studies.

The Lord gave me strength, and in a number of different ways I managed to obtain the necessary money to cover my costs. From a distance the brothers and sisters continued to support me, while those who remained at CONEP also encouraged me. So bit by bit I became familiar with the work and finally stayed on to work with CONEP.

God gave me the opportunity to revisit Huancayo Prison and to encourage those who are still there. I know that my work is not over and that God has still more great things planned for me.

## Notes

1   The term "criado" refers to a boy or girl who is taken into the home of a relative or friend. They work as a domestic servant in return for food, clothing and education. They do not receive a salary.

2   The presence of Peruvian anti-drug forces, along with the support of the US DEA, dedicated to combating narco-trafficking, and crop substitution programmes, has substantially reduced this activity.

# CHAPTER FOUR

# PELAGIA

Pelagia lived in Vilcashuamán, Ayacucho, where she was born, until she was 20. She completed her elementary studies but was unable to continue with her education as most of her time was taken up by her farming responsibilities and looking after the livestock. Her life continued in a simple, orderly way until her sixteenth birthday, when she married Juan Carlos.

She and Juan Carlos stayed in Vilcashuamán, where they devoted themselves totally to farming. By 1980, however, when the Shining Path began its armed uprising in Ayacucho, they were living in the village of San Francisco.

The main objective of the Shining Path was to eliminate all community leaders and social organisations in an effort to provoke chaos. They believed that this would then allow them to establish themselves as the rebel leaders of a revolution, which would, according to them, bring about a new society.

Juan Carlos was a community leader in San Francisco. His position brought him to the attention of the Shining Path in 1981. He received a number of threats, and when another one of the community leaders was assassinated he realised that he had to flee to Lima. It was a spur-of-the-moment decision. He had never been to the capital, but he knew someone who went there regularly and asked him for directions.

Pelagia stayed behind in San Francisco until the next harvest. Four months after Juan Carlos's departure she too made the journey to the capital, taking her young son with her.

To start with the family stayed with Juan Carlos's cousin in the suburb of El Callao, but in 1982 they took over a piece of land in Canto Grande and moved there to make their own home. Pelagia concentrated on selling sweets in the market while Juan Carlos worked on building their house. As he was a skilled builder, he constructed their house swiftly.

Canto Grande is located in the district of San Juan de Lurigancho, in the eastern "cone", or impoverished outskirts, of Lima. The area is densely populated by people who for the most part have come from the Andes and other poverty-stricken provinces of Peru.

Canto Grande was settled by continuous waves of migrants who arrived in Lima along the Central Highway. The same approach was used by the Shining Path, who came to Lima as part of a "countryside-to-town" strategy. Because of this, the National Intelligence Service began studying Canto Grande in 1992 and 1993, and conducted continuous military *rastrillajes*[1] or raids there.

Beginning in 1992, the new government under Alberto Fujimori initiated an anti-subversive policy, utilising the military in an effort to wipe out terrorist activity. On 5th April of the same year the government, supported by the armed forces, shut down the civil branches of government, including Congress and the judiciary. That done, Fujimori declared an Emergency Government for National Reconstruction. From then on, raids took place more frequently.

In the meantime, since the family had left Ayacucho,

Pelagia's life had developed naturally along its new course in Lima. In 1986 she became an evangelical Christian at a World Missionary Movement church in La Victoria district. In 1984 her daughter Marlene was born, and a new and happy stage of her life began. This lasted until the night of 11th December 1992, when a group of about 20 soldiers arrested her and her husband. They were accused of being members of the Shining Path.

People living in Lima's cones were regularly detained so that their personal possessions and documents could be inspected. If they lived in the eastern cone, and if it was discovered that they originally came from Ayacucho, there was all the more reason to detain them and take them to a military base. Once there, everything depended on the frame of mind of the official in charge. Hardly anyone emerged from the experience without receiving at the very least threats or a beating. To be from Ayacucho, like Pelagia and Juan Carlos, was to be a terrorist suspect.

Pelagia's testimony shows how the inner workings of the raids were kept secret and how the term *rastrillaje* was a euphemism hiding the fact that the military or the police abused the many innocent people they dealt with. The prospect of promotion was a tempting incentive that often outweighed conscience in members of the security forces.

Pelagia tells the story of her detention and the years she spent wrongly imprisoned in the following lines.

# 1

We were woken up by the noise of someone walking on our roof. It was 3:00 am and, thinking that it might be burglars, I shouted out: "What is happening? Who's up there?"

After a brief silence we heard a loud voice call out, "Stay

where you are – it's the police. Nobody move, otherwise we'll shoot you all right now!"

When we went out into the hallway we were surrounded by about 20 policemen. "No talking! Get out on the patio, all of you!" shouted one of them.

They pushed my husband to one side of the house, gagged him and bound him. They forced me up against the wall. "Don't move! Look straight ahead! Do what we say or we'll kill you!"

I was now in tears. The whole situation seemed like a nightmare to me. Their next move was to take my children out of their bedrooms. They treated them the same way, gagging them and pushing them up against the wall.

My little daughter was crying piteously. "Mummy, why is all this happening? Why have these policemen come? Have you done something wrong?"

I did not understand what was happening, and I said to one of the men, "Sergeant, why are you doing this to us? What do you want to find in our house?"

Because I carried on so much a policeman said to me, "Señora, we are carrying out a *rastrillaje*. Just do what we tell you to do!"

This made me a little calmer. If this was true, well, we were not hiding anything. In addition, during that period this sort of raid was very common, especially after there had been an assassination attempt.

After turning our house over and searching through everything for about two hours, a policeman came out with something in his hand, shouting, "So, they were pretending to be innocent, were they? Look, mate, these people are from Ayacucho; they *must* be terrorists."

"But there isn't anything in this house to prove that," one of the others objected.

Their leader said tersely, "Don't worry about proof; that can easily be arranged, but we have to keep searching; there must be *something* here."

They continued to search for another half-hour and then one of them said to me, "Señora, you need to help us look now, because who knows your house better than you do?"

"You have been searching yourself and have found nothing. Everything has been taken out and is on view," I replied indignantly.

"Do as you're told or we'll give you a good beating," he repeated, irritated.

We went into my bedroom and then into the kitchen and then into the yard. They found nothing. Then we went out into the yard at the side of the house. As we came outside we saw three policemen sitting round a mound of sand that we had been using to build our house. I saw them take a black bag out of it, pretending to pull it out from underneath.

"Señora, what's this, then?"

"That bag wasn't there before," I said.

"Don't be naïve. If you live here you would know about everything on your property, wouldn't you?"

They began to take various metal implements out of the bag. I realised that they were guns and other weapons.

Very indignant, I said to them between sobs, "Why are you doing this to us? We have never had those things in our house. You brought all those things here because you knew you wouldn't find anything. Anyway, if they had really been under that sand, as you say, the bag wouldn't be so clean."

This rattled them badly. "Don't act the innocent with us, Señora. Your whimpering is of no use here, nor are the stupid things you're saying. We found this here and that's the end of it. This was obviously a place for training other terrorists to kill a lot of innocent people!"

They began to harass me. "What do you call this? If there are weapons in your house it must be because you're terrorists. You know full well what's going on, don't you?"

One of them tried to force me to pick up one of the weapons. When I refused and shook my head he seized me by the hair and I had to pick it up. Right then one of the other officers took photographs of me.

They brought my husband out and took off his gag. When he saw the weapons he passed out. As he lay there, unconscious, they began beating and insulting him. "Terrorist! You had a whole collection of things here, didn't you?"

He was beaten back into consciousness. He asked for water but they would not let me get anything for him. I was only able to do so a long while afterwards.

They took all the things into the living room, put the weapons on the table and took several photographs. Then they tried to make us sign a sheet of paper but they would not allow us to read what it said. I only managed to make out: "These people are terrorists and we have found weapons in this house".

When I refused to sign it, they jammed a gun against my head. "You will sign or we'll kill you!" one of them kept on.

My little girl was frightened and said to me, "Mummy, sign it, or they're going to kill you."

"Flaca, don't sign anything," my husband said to me.

As he said that they began to beat him, and as they did so someone seized my hand and forced me to sign.

At about 6:00 am they took us out of the house. They did not allow us to say goodbye to our children. They drove us to DINCOTE, where another group of policemen received us, treating us as if we were criminals. They insulted us and brought out other pieces of paper stating that we were terrorists, which they tried to force us to sign. When we denied that we were terrorists they threatened to go and get our children.

We were forced to sign, under duress, and then they separated us from each other. They took me to the women's cells.

And that's how my imprisonment began. For a week I prayed to the Lord and told him of my longing to read his Word. I knew that he had heard my plea when the policeman who had arrested us told me that my brother-in-law had sent me something. It was my Bible.

"You don't understand how much I need it. It contains the Word of God, which has given us so much courage and consolation," I told him.

"You're obviously here because you're a terrorist, and now you are claiming to be religious to catch us off guard."

I did not say anything to him in reply. I just prayed and asked the Lord to soften his heart. Three days later he returned. "Señora Pelagia, here's your Bible. I don't care that you're lying to me; hopefully the Bible will change you."

That afternoon was beautiful. I read Psalm 51 and later I met Antonia, another prisoner. She was also a believer and, although she could not read, we shared the Word together. We asked God to release us and for protection for our families.

One afternoon, as I was reading the Bible, two young women from the Shining Path approached me.

"Pelagia, I don't understand how you can believe in something that does not exist. God does not exist. You are regressing in all aspects. You should try to advance in other areas and get to know a little more of the real world."

"There is nothing more important than God to me. We will never find peace through violence. God does not like war and bloodshed," I told them.

"But we want to know where your God is. What you read in your Bible is all lies. You should be participating in the struggle."

I simply replied that the period of violence and death

through which we were living was foretold in the Bible as "the sign of the last days", like the coming of the Lord Jesus.

Life inside prison was very difficult. We were not given any food and had to rely on our families to bring us breakfast, lunch and dinner. Many prisoners had no family, so we shared what we had with some of them.

My husband had been assigned to the third floor but sometimes he came down to the second to give me words of courage and consolation. "Keep calm, Pelagia, because we are innocent. We are not involved in any of this. Man can say many things but it is God who will make everything clear."

"But our children are all alone!" I replied.

"I'm thinking about them, too, but God has not abandoned us. He is with them," he said encouragingly.

Our family found a lawyer who tried to help us, but the authorities threatened to kill him and told him that if he defended terrorists he would be considered to be one too. Then another lawyer came along, but although we spent a lot of money he was unable to do anything to help us.

Eventually they told us that we would be handed over to the civil authorities. Another one of the prisoners, however, told us that they said that to everyone in an effort to stop us from worrying, but that in the end we would be handed over to the military.

A policeman came to transfer us to another prison. As he did so he asked why we were there if we were really innocent, and who had brought us there. When we said that Captain Renates was responsible, he said, "Renates treats people with every injustice imaginable. He has clearly made a mistake, because you should not be here."

We were taken to the Palace of Justice. They asked us some questions while we were there, then we signed some documents and once again we were separated. They took me back to the Santa Mónica Prison with other women. On the way, I became very distraught because of what the other women said to me. "At Santa Mónica they will beat you and mistreat you. The other prisoners will take everything you have."

All this distressed me greatly, but I prayed to the Lord and asked him to soften the hearts of those whom I would meet there.

## II

On my first day in prison I felt horrible. The other prisoners gave me strange looks. A bold young woman came up to me and said, "You must be the leader of some party cell. You might as well tell us everything because nothing leaves this place."

"You are wrong; I'm only here because of some mix-up. Everything that has been done to me was unjust. God will soon set me free," I replied.

On the following day I spoke to the captain. "Good morning, Captain. May I ask you a favour? I'm innocent and I do not want to be held together with the women from the Shining Path. I have been placed here unjustly."

"Don't worry, Señora, because there are others like you here and I am going to put you together with them," he replied.

I felt very happy and I thanked the Lord for this blessing. I was taken to join other prisoners, many of whom I had known from the prison where I had been held before. But once again I had difficulties getting my Bible in.

"Señora, I am only carrying out orders, and nobody is allowed to bring in any type of book," the captain said to me.

When the colonel came, I asked him if I could have my Bible and hymn book.

"What's that?" he asked me. "It must contain terrorist teachings."

"No, Colonel! It is the Word of God!"

"Yes, but the Bible is also being used for other purposes."

I explained to him that I needed it only to receive Christ's message and to praise the Lord, but the colonel would not agree.

The following day I persisted. "Colonel, please give me my Bible."

"Señora, calm yourself, because at least you are in a safe place here."

As he walked away I prayed to the Lord, "Touch his heart, soften his spirit; it is not right that they have taken away my Bible."

When I opened my eyes I saw him coming back.

"Señora, does your Bible have your name written in it?"

"No, there isn't anything written in my Bible, but my name is written in my hymn book," I replied.

After a few minutes the colonel returned with both of my books.

The other prisoners, who had seen the whole thing, were left speechless. "Pelagia, you are special! No one is ever allowed so much as a piece of paper in here!"

"This has happened thanks to the Lord," I replied.

On the following day I resumed my reading. I praised and sang to the Lord, particularly a chorus which says:

> I have decided to follow Jesus
> The cross before me,
> The world behind me . . .
> No turning back,
> No turning back.

After a month I was taken before the court in Castro Castro Prison, the same prison in which my husband was being held.

They sent me into a large hall, where he was already waiting. We had no defence prepared whatsoever. Suddenly we heard a voice, but we could not see anyone.

"They are the faceless judges," a woman explained to me.

Suddenly the same voice rang out again. "Carlos Chuchón and Pelagia Salcedo. You are sentenced to life imprisonment. Do you agree to the sentence?"

We were stupefied, speechless, confused.

The duty lawyer came up. "Señora, they are asking you if you accept the sentence."

"How can you think that I would agree to a sentence for something we haven't done?" I replied. I began to cry, and added, "This isn't fair; we aren't guilty of anything."

"But Señora, we can always appeal against this judgement," the lawyer said to me.

My husband broke his silence: "This is an injustice; it cannot be allowed! We have not committed any crime. We are not terrorists; we are Christians."

I went to console him. I told him to be calm, that our God was just and was going to free us from all this. We had to trust in him. He knew that we were innocent and was not going to allow us to spend such a long time in prison.

When we said goodbye to each other, we were calmer. The whole experience was extremely difficult. If the Lord had not given us strength at that moment, it is possible that we might have chosen suicide.

When we got back to Santa Mónica Prison one of the prisoners wanted to know what had happened to us. "Tell us, Pelagia, you've been freed, haven't you?"

"There is no justice here. They have passed sentence on me," I said.

"Sentenced you? It's not possible! You are innocent!"

I told her that I was calm, that I had begun to rest in the

Lord. That he was just and would very soon take me away from all this.

"They have sentenced you to life imprisonment and yet you speak so calmly, as if you were just here for a week," said another prisoner.

"It's true; I ought to be on the verge of suicide. But thanks to the strength that God gives me I can retain this serenity that astonishes you," I added.

On the following day I read Psalm 102, and the passage in Luke 18 that speaks of a just God who will give justice to his chosen who call on him night and day. This made me remember, "God knows that I am innocent and I trust that he will give us justice."

One morning as I was reading the Bible, someone said to me, "There's another crazy woman like you who does nothing but read the Bible in the next cell. Her name is Amavel."

They called us crazy because they said that we believed in something that did not exist.

I met Amavel one day when we went out onto the patio. We talked, and upon recognising that we were sisters in the faith we embraced and cried with happiness. From that point on we sought each other out to share the Word of God and to pray together. We prayed for freedom, for the protection of our families and for the authorities in the prison. Then, little by little, we met other Christian women. The first was sister Curi, next Yolanda and then Santosa. Now we were five. We gathered together to sing, pray and read the Word of God.
A hymn that we sang said:

> I found a good friend, my belovèd Saviour.
> I shall tell what he has done for me.
> He found me a lost and unworthy sinner and
>   today he keeps me for his own;

He saves me from sin,
He shields me from Satan,
He promises to be with me until the end.
He comforts my sorrow,
Takes away all anxiety;
Christ has done great things for me.
Jesus never lets me down; he will never abandon me;
He is my strong and powerful protector.
He keeps me from the world and vanity so that
    I can consecrate my life to the Lord.
If the world pursues me, if I suffer temptation,
If I trust in Christ I can resist.
Alleluia! I am assured of victory and I lift up my
    voice in song,
Christ has done great things for me.

When the other Christians in the prison heard about our meetings, the group grew. The example of the Apostle Paul, who also sang and prayed even when he was imprisoned, was a great inspiration for us. Many other prisoners did not understand what our faith was. But still others were made free in Jesus.

My family were only able to visit me once a month and then only for 25 or 30 minutes. My sister-in-law always came and brought me news of my husband, who was still being held in Castro Castro Prison.

My little daughter inspired me greatly; she told me I would soon be free. "Mama, trust in God, and don't lose hope. I am praying for your freedom and so are the brothers and sisters in all the churches."

That gave me a good deal of strength. Now I did not feel so alone. However, my little son was always quiet and suffering inside. It was lovely to see my family; they brought me so much joy, but the 30 minutes passed quickly and then the sadness returned.

One day I received a beautiful letter from my husband, brought from the Yanamayo Prison in Puno by brother Vinces, a lawyer from Paz y Esperanza:

My dear Wife,

I pray that you are in good health in the company of your sisters in the prison. I am still well, thanks to our Sovereign God, Jehovah. I continue to study his Word. You know, Flaca, I received your letter. But, my dear wife, I was saddened to see that you only have a small piece of paper of some ten centimetres on which to write to me. I advise you to use whatever little piece of white material you can find. When one knows the Word of God one loves one's neighbour and his wife, true? (Matt 22:39). Because love covers a multitude of sins (1 Peter 4:8). But one must cast off the old man and put on the new (Col. 3: 8–10).

Please study the Bible regularly so that you may better understand the truth, because the truth will set us free (John 8:32). And please tell our children to behave well at all times. If Jehovah God is willing, we shall soon leave here, and you and I will go out preaching the Word of God from house to house. Then our home will be filled with happiness. Believe me, Flaca, I love you very much and I cherish you with Christian love. You know, don't you, that it is not easy to be a Christian, because many of the other men make fun of me here in the prison and even insult me. These people do not believe in God.

I send you my affectionate greetings, a kiss and a big hug. Greetings also to my little sisters who are studying the Bible and seeking God by truly meditating on his Word. Speak to la Negra also and to Aurelio to get them to go to the meetings, so that they too may know the truth. Until we meet again, and take good care of yourself.

Juan Carlos Chuchón Zea.

PS: I received the jumper that you sent me. Thank you.

Meeting the other Christian women in the prison was a lovely experience. It was very comforting to praise God together with them in prison. It gave me great joy. My heart was full. Before this I had felt all alone.

I had always found it difficult to understand the Word of God. I had consistently asked the Lord to bring me someone who knew the Bible, and so it was that I met Amavel. I asked her about the things I did not understand and she explained them to me.

We wanted to meet more frequently but we had to ask the colonel, who thought we had an ulterior motive. For that reason we always prayed that they would bring other sisters to us from the other cellblocks. And so, gradually, the colonel brought them over one by one to our block. They wanted to be with us, too.

According to the prison rules during that period, children could visit only every three months, so my daughter, Marlene, visited me that often. My son, Abilio, however, only came to see me twice. Both times he came he did not say a word, but only looked at me, his eyes welling up with tears. After the second time he never came back to the prison again. My sister-in-law told me that after Abilio came to see me he refused to eat, had headaches and complained of feeling ill.

My son was very afraid because he had been there when the police arrested us. They had tied him up and blindfolded him. They had traumatised him.

Marlene was able to begin to overcome her trauma because she was going to a church near where they lived. She met others there and studied the Bible with them. They gave her the strength to overcome what had happened to her. My son, however, was unable to do this. Because they had given us a life sentence, which was later reduced to 30 years, he held on to this idea that we would never get out of prison.

During the first few months in prison we suffered a great deal because of the low quality of the food. It was brought from INPE (the National Penitentiary Institution) and it was rotten and dirty. But what could we do? I prayed to God and asked him not to let that food make me ill. The utensils were very dirty when they arrived and there were even beetles and stones in the food.

Thanks to God, the colonel took care of the situation. He managed to get a stove installed in the cellblock. From that point on we did our own cooking, and the food improved markedly. We had two rolls and a cup of oats for breakfast and for lunch we would eat a bowl or two of soup. We had lunch at 1:00 or 2:00 in the afternoon. Before this happened there had been no fixed mealtime; sometimes we would not eat until 5:00 or 6:00 in the evening.

At the beginning of my stay there I spent my time making felt dolls and knitting jumpers on some machines that had been donated to the prison. I made jumpers for my children and to sell in order to provide some income for them. My aunt would take the jumpers and sell them on the outside for me.

Sometimes I lost all hope of ever walking out as a free woman, and even began to ask God why he had forgotten me. During my first few years in prison armed violence was shaking the entire country and we heard that the government had announced that terrorist prisoners would never leave prison. It was very difficult to be so unjustly accused, but the Word of God always spoke to me and I clung to him more and more.

I prayed, "Lord, they can say anything about me, but you know my heart. You know what I am going through . . ." and I always continued to pray. At that time there was no legal procedure that would allow a review of our cases. There was no talk of pardon or anything of the sort.

## III

And so the months passed. After three years had passed, a lawyer who had begun to review my case came to see me and said, "Señora, your case is very difficult. We have presented some documents for review but the case has been closed. There is nothing else we can do."

He was very sad but I felt strengthened spiritually. "Don't worry, Doctor, I know something will happen. I am going to pray to the Lord and ask him to show the way. He will not abandon me."

"Others lose heart but you give me courage, Señora," he said, smiling.

The lawyer returned two months later and told me that the Pardoning Law had been passed. I thought to myself that the Lord was beginning to show himself.

One Thursday the assistant from the IDL (Legal Defence Institute) who regularly visited us came and told us what was happening on the outside. She brought enough material for me to work on my felt dolls. I thought that as I was not going to get out I had enough work to last me for a good long while.

The following day I got up early to do my chores. It was about half past six when the colonel came. "Señora, get ready to go!"

"Don't play games, Colonel! It's very wrong of you to do that to me," I replied.

"Ah, Señora, you don't want to leave? Well, then you can stay here."

He walked away, but before he reached the door I asked, "Is it true, Colonel?"

"Yes, Señora, you really are getting out," he replied, smiling.

At that moment the official began calling out the names of

other Christian women, and our entire group of evangelical Christians left together. God listens to all our requests.

We evangelicals were always ostracised in the prison. Both the prisoners and the authorities mocked us. We had prayed that we would all be chosen together, and sisters Santosa, Antonia, Celedonia, Liduvina and I left together. That day was like waking from a long sleep. My husband was also released from Yanamayo Prison at the same time. God had done this.

I clearly remember 4th October 1996, when I was released, thanks to the Pardoning Commission's intervention.

On my release I found that my children had changed a great deal. Each had their own life. They had been deeply affected by four years without me. At the beginning my son Abilio felt uncomfortable whenever he was with us. He saw us only at mealtimes, then he would shut himself up in his room or go out into the street.

When we were imprisoned my children were sent to live with their uncle and aunt in Los Olivos. Now we live together, but we cannot return to our house in Canto Grande. When we were in prison the house was confiscated by the Military Tribunal and when we were released they gave it back to us, but the place brings back too many terrible memories.

At the present time we attend the Assemblies of God Church and we have overcome much of the trauma we suffered during our four years in prison. Our family has reintegrated itself. Abilio is working and studying mechanics in the SENATI, and now talks to us more. Marlene has resumed her secondary studies and God has blessed us with a new son. This son marks the beginning of a new life for my family.

# Note

1 A *rastrillaje* was a joint police and military surprise operation during which neighbourhoods were blocked off. The
authorities would then register the residents, inspect
private property and often raze homes to the ground in an
effort to smoke out terrorist elements. On a number of
occasions the military used these *rastrillajes* as an opportunity to plant evidence in order to link individuals to subversive activities.

# CHAPTER FIVE

# SAÚL

Saúl had always had a particular talent for mathematics. Born in Lima in December 1968, he later studied at Independence College in the district of the same name. During his final year at the college he made a decision to follow Christ at the Baptist Bible Church of El Ermitaño. His father worked for the Ministry of Health and his mother was a housewife.

In 1982, after a year and a half of preparation, Saúl entered the National University of Engineering (UNI) where he specialised in mechanical engineering, a subject that fascinated him. His joy was shared by his parents and his six brothers and sisters.

Like many other Peruvians, Saúl carried a number of responsibilities in addition to his studies. This meant that his pursuit of a degree did not follow the most straightforward course. In 1985 he was contracted as head of trigonometry testing at the Alfa Academy.[1] He worked there for one and a half years, balancing his work as a lecturer with his engineering studies.

In 1986, as a birthday gift, he received news that he was being offered a position as lecturer at the Cesar Vallejo Academy. This academy was the only one that held a competition for lecturers and that year he had competed with scores of professors, mainly from the UNI and San Marcos.

Saúl continued to alternate between his work as a lecturer and his own university studies. At the university he regularly overheard political discussions, and every once in a while he heard people utter Shining Path slogans. He took part in a few of these discussions, explaining his point of view as a Christian, but he never aligned himself with any particular political position. In addition, his university department was not known for being very politically minded. The debates on political development took place for the most part in the university dining hall.

The same type of political discourse was also developing at the academy, but Saúl kept his distance from all of this, as his main concern was simply to be a good lecturer. In addition, almost all of his colleagues were aware that he was a practising evangelical.

In 1992 the academy began to experience political problems as the administration was covertly taken over by members of the Shining Path. The police began an investigation which resulted in the imprisonment of about 30 people, including fellows and directors. Consequently the academy was left with no effective administration, although more than two thousand students continued to attend classes.

Saúl had completed a number of years at the academy as an effective lecturer, and this was acknowledged by many of his colleagues. As a result, the new administration offered him the position of financial secretary at the academy. At first he rejected the offer because of the high level of responsibility that came with it, but, after they insisted, he accepted the job. Because of this new responsibility Saúl was later asked by the Peruvian courts to testify in the cases against the academy fellows accused of terrorism.

He began his work as financial secretary in July of that year, and at first everything went well. The academy generated a huge income and the administration planned to buy an additional piece of land in order to construct new facilities.

At first the new administrators distanced themselves from all discussion regarding the Shining Path. This went on until a group of fellows tried to take over the academy again under the name of the Communist Party of Peru of the Shining Path. They asked Saúl to support them, but he refused. As a result they threatened him and applied severe pressure, until finally he was forced to renounce his post. The group of fellows replaced him with another, more loyal, person.

As he had no alternative he surrendered his position as financial secretary, but he requested that they completely remove his name from the staff registries as he did not want to be involuntarily implicated in anything they did from that point on. He was, however, allowed to continue in his post as lecturer.

Simultaneously, the same group also began to put pressure on the president of the directors – who then opted to remove the fellows who were causing the problem. This decision was made in January 1993 in the face of protest from a small group of fellows. They attempted to hold on to their positions but the president stood his ground and threw them out. This, in turn, provoked their ire, and they decided to resort to other methods to achieve their objectives.

A few days after the incident, the Shining Path's regional commander for the metropolitan area of Lima paid a visit to the academy. His objective was to coerce the president into reinstating the expelled fellows. The Shining Path commander entered with one of his deputies. They seized the president and took him into a classroom, where they handcuffed him and began to assault him.

Saúl, indignant at this outrage, attempted to get into the classroom in order to challenge the invaders, but he was prevented from doing so. After a prolonged effort he managed to enter the classroom and reprimanded the Shining Path member for his presence and actions there. Immediately the commander turned and began to spout a mass of ideological propaganda similar to that which Saúl would later hear regularly in prison.

After this the president of the academy was virtually paralysed. Later the vice-president sacked the entire administration and took complete control of the academy. This new president was well known for his ambition and appeared to have no problem accepting the demands of the Shining Path in dictating the principles of the academy and how it should be run.

In March 1993 the new president and a number of other "directors", whom nobody had known about but who had clandestinely governed the academy, were detained by the authorities. Some of these individuals took advantage of the Repentance Law and denounced a number of their other colleagues at the academy.

Although the group of fellows involved with the Shining Path were removed from their posts at the academy, Saúl decided not to resume his duties as financial secretary and dedicated himself to his work as a lecturer. He was thinking about resigning and collecting his compensation when, in August of the same year, upon leaving one of his classes, he was detained by the police.

It appeared that his name had never been erased from the list of directors as he had requested. Instead, one of the Shining Path members had completely taken over the administration of the money and had used Saúl's name as a façade behind which to hide their activities. Saúl did not have a single document with which to prove his innocence, and after a military trial he was condemned to 20 years in prison.

On 29th October 1997 Saúl was freed after the intervention of the Ad Hoc Commission of Pardons and through the support of Peace and Hope. By the second half of 1998 he was able to finish his civil engineering studies thanks to the help of the university administration, and he now works for the Ministry of Health on various paid projects.

Saúl tells the story of his period of imprisonment below.

# I

Everything began the night of 21st August 1993, when I returned to the Cesar Vallejo Academy with my brother and a colleague. I was a professor there and also worked in administration. At the same time I was studying at the university. That night we were stopped by three policemen.

"Which one of you is Saúl Tito Coicca?"

"I am," I responded immediately.

At that moment they grabbed me and pointed a gun at my head. They forced me into a dilapidated car, put a sack over the upper half of my body and began to beat me. They told me that I must have all the university's money and if I would just cooperate with them they would help me out.

I told them that I was just a professor and that they could look through my bags, but as I was an evangelical they would find only a Bible.

"Sure, now you're saying you're a 'brother' to hide your guilt," they sneered.

They searched me and didn't find anything, but they forced me into the car boot anyway. I felt as though they were not treating me like a living being. I turned my thoughts to the Lord, prayed and felt his presence there with me. "I want to be with you and I will face this situation head on. Lord, please help me," I asked.

Next they took me out of the boot and drove me to a house where another group of policemen began to interrogate me.

"Look, skinny boy, cooperate with us or you're done for. Do you know Feliciano?"

They showed me a number of photos – including one of Abimael Guzman.[2]

"Do you know where Abimael is?"

I did not recognise anyone in the photos, except for Abimael.

"You are questioning me as if I belonged to the Shining Path. I'm a Christian and I don't have anything to do with them," I answered.

They became impatient and started to maltreat me. They pulled my hands behind my back and started to beat me. After a few blows, they sat on me, pushing down hard.

"Please, no!" I cried out.

"Then speak!" they shouted.

I told them that I didn't know anything about any of this – that I was an evangelical, that I had no political leanings, that I didn't know much about what was going on in the country and that teaching at the academy did not automatically mean that I was a terrorist.

"But you know that there are members of the Shining Path there!"

"I know, but even though they tried to pressure me I haven't compromised any of my Christian principles. The Bible you found in my bag is proof of my faith in Christ."

When they heard this, they stopped hitting me.

At that point I spoke to the Lord. "I don't have anything to hide; I leave everything in your hands; I know that you will accompany me."

The interrogation and the beatings had begun at 10:00 at night and finished at 1:00 in the morning.

Next I was put in the care of a policeman. My head was covered. He asked me to show my hands and then he hit me with a metal key, which left my fingers numb. I began to understand that he wanted me to give him some money.

After this I had to speak with some other officials. Things became even more difficult with them. They asked me for information that I simply couldn't give them. When I told them I didn't know anything, they hit me. I was much thinner then, and my body was unable to withstand some of the blows that it received. They were blows such as I had never experienced in my life. I felt as if they had broken my waist in half. Every now and then they would stop hitting me long enough to ask me more questions. They showed me more photos of people I didn't know and, since they didn't believe me when I told them so, they continued to beat me.

After repeated beatings they pretended to present me to the press. They wanted to see how I would react. They brought cameras and fake journalists and presented me to them as Comrade Tito. They told them that I was the number three leader in the Shining Path and that I was the head of the logistical apparatus at the Cesar Vallejo Academy. They said that I was carrying a fake electoral book because it didn't have my second last name listed in it. They insisted that Tito was not a surname and they told me to call my lawyer.

"Surely it's a democratic lawyer!"

I didn't understand what they were referring to when they talked about a "democratic lawyer".

This was all a set-up, but even then I was very passive and did not react the way that they had hoped I would. I remember that I even started to smile, because in the midst of all that pain my strength was in the Lord. I thought that if I did not emerge from this bitter experience alive, I knew where I was going to be.

After this farce, they made me go through a kind of medical examination. The doctor just greeted me with, "That's all, go ahead, there's no more", without even looking over my body.

They drove me to the dungeons of DINCOTE, cell sixteen on the first floor. This cell was two metres by two metres, with five people crammed inside. I slept standing up the first night because there was no space on the floor of the cell.

I wasn't allowed to see any visitors for three days. On the third day a policeman appeared and told me I could go home to see my family.

"Am I free?" I asked excitedly.

"You've still got a long way to go, buddy," he said. "We have to search your house now and see if we can find anything there that we don't already know about from your declarations."

After we arrived at my house I hugged my mother and my sisters. Crying, my mother said to the policeman, "What you are doing to my son is unjust. He doesn't have anything to do with terrorists. He's an honest boy, dedicated to our Lord Jesus Christ."

"Calm down, madam," they answered. "He's OK. We just want to ask a few questions. If he really doesn't have anything to do with it, he'll be freed."

After examining the entire house, they took away only a few photos of me playing sports at work. Afterwards they took me back to the dungeons.

When we arrived, the policeman asked me who I was.

"I am Saúl Tito Coicca and I was captured because I was a professor at the Cesar Vallejo Academy. I know that there were some professors arrested there who were involved with the Shining Path, but I never had anything to do with them."

"Look, skinny boy, we've reviewed your case and you're not really part of our plans, but now that you're here we have to finish the investigation. You have one thing in your favour: so far you've behaved yourself well and you've cooperated with us."

I was disconcerted to be back inside prison but I did not lose my confidence in the Lord. I was surprised to hear a group of prisoners singing praise songs that I recognised. I went over to them and listened to one of the brothers preach about not losing faith in God. He said that wherever we were, he would always be at our side. We sang a chorus inspired by Joshua 1:9: "This is my command: be strong, be resolute; do not be fearful or discouraged, for wherever you go the Lord your God is with you."

We finished the meeting and one of them came over and introduced himself.

"Hi, I'm Juan Malléa. Welcome to the church of the Lord," he said to me.

"I'm Saúl Tito. What a pleasure it is to meet you, Juan. I know all about you from reading the newspapers. Everyone says that you are innocent."

## II

Seven days later, on 24th October, I was transferred to the Castro Castro Prison. They transferred three hundred of the accused in just one bus. We travelled practically on top of one another and were almost asphyxiated.

After a stupendous beating I was installed in cell twelve in Cellblock 5A.

In Castro Castro Prison Colonel Cajahuanca told us that he wanted to help the Christians. "Who here believes in God?"

Juan, Simon, Darwin and I raised our hands.

"You can go out onto the patio."

"Thank you, Colonel," we said immediately.

We began a process of integration within the group that we formed and between praise songs and hymns we managed to grow in the Lord. I often remember the first hymn we sang: "There is no God as great as you; There is no God that can work like you work. It is not with the sword or with an army but by your Holy Spirit."

The guards were taken aback by what we were doing. One of them challenged us, saying, "Let's see, then, I want to see your God get you out of here. A lot of men become Christians inside here, but, tomorrow in the streets, they return to being terrorists."

The Lord filled us with a spirit of understanding in all of this. We rested in him without responding, and just continued to praise God.

Two weeks later, Colonel Cajahuanca's attitude towards me changed. One day he came over and began to abuse me. He threatened to send me to the "Hole", a punishment cell, because a group of subversives that had been expelled from the Cesar Vallejo Academy had apparently told an official that I was the leader of the imprisoned group from the academy. He threatened to send me to Yanamayo[3] and ordered the guards to watch me constantly. He announced that I was a Shining Path member, particularly dangerous, and he took photos of me so that all the guards would know who I was. The tension died down after a few days, however, when he realised that I was just a human being, and a peaceful one at that.

In the prison we were supposed to have been given some kind of instructions about our legal situations. Unfortunately, however, this process never took place, which meant that I missed the opportunity to clear up my case.

At my first hearing before a judge I was taken out with a group of other men who were also accused of terrorism. I felt remorseful and powerless, as if I were actually part of a bunch of bloodthirsty delinquents. There were more policemen than accused in the room.

After a brief silence, a voice rang out from behind a window of about ten by two metres. "Saúl Tito Coicca. You are accused of trying to rescue Abimael Guzman from the Callao Naval Base and of giving logistical support to the Shining Path."

My family had hired a lawyer to represent me. In our second meeting he told me, "Saúl, we know that you are innocent, but tell me about the money from the academy. I have to know about it in order to defend you. How is it possible that you could be in charge of so much money and not take a little for yourself?"

I told him that he sounded like a police lawyer and that I would not even consider attempting to get out of prison under the "Repentance Law" because this would mean admitting that I had been part of the Shining Path.

"I can repent of my sins and my mistakes before God. And perhaps one of these mistakes was to remain at the academy. But I cannot repent of something that I did not do," I concluded.

I had very little confidence in him, because he did not believe me. I prayed to God and as I did so it occurred to me that there was a lot of work to be done in the prisons, and somebody had to do it. As I reflected on this I wondered, "What do I do here?" and the answer I received was, "God has put me here and has strengthened me, and the pain and the sadness I feel now will be converted into happiness and even more love for my neighbour."

One day, at about 2:00 in the afternoon, they took me out

of my cell and put me before a judge, along with the other accused. We entered one by one. When it was my turn, I answered each question clearly, as I rested in the Lord.

"Did you know Juan Suazo and Mirta Simon?"

"Yes, they were teachers at the academy," I answered.

"And Mr Limaco?"

"No, I don't know that one," I said.

These audiences took place over four months. The time went by very quickly. At the final session, after ten previous presentations before the "faceless judge", we waited until 7:00 in the evening to hear the sentences.

"Mr Saúl Tito Coicca, alias 'Comrade Tito', you are sentenced to 20 years in prison."

This unexpected news pained me deeply. I felt a great deal of anguish, and cried, "God, you have given me so much to cope with, and now you are allowing this to happen?"

Later, however, I looked to the Lord and said inside myself, "Lord, if this is your will I will continue to work as I have been doing, and I will plant and build and I will demonstrate that they were wrong to do this."

As they took me back to the prison I caught sight of my mother. She was crying and I said, "Lord, please look upon the pain of my mother and console her in this moment." I wept myself to see her so close to me and me unable to wipe the tears from her face. They put me into a car and my mother, unable to follow, got lost in the distance.

Back in the prison, the other men wanted to know what had happened.

"They sentenced me to 20 years. They didn't even want to hear my arguments," I told them.

That first Christmas in prison was a gloomy time – but in spite of the circumstances the brothers all wanted to spend it together. I directed the group. We celebrated Christmas with the will to do so as best we could, but it took a lot out of us to say "Happy Christmas".

### III

The group of brothers was growing. We were winning the goodwill of the authorities but it was not easy. There was a lot of pressure coming from the prisoners who were affiliated to the subversive groups. In addition, at times one was unable to speak freely. It was impossible to know who the people with whom we spoke really were. It was easy to doubt a brother. Some of them seemed overly reserved.

In the middle of 1995, God sent the lawyers Ruth Alvarado and José Vinces, both Christians, to us. My family had been contacted by the brothers and sisters at Peace and Hope of CONEP and had managed to speak with evangelical lawyers who fought for justice.

"Your family told us about your case. We are putting together some documents to get permission to talk with you personally. In addition, many Christians all over the world are praying for you."

I was overcome by emotion and felt deeply comforted at hearing this. Afterwards, brother José Regalado, another lawyer from CONEP, was able to come and meet with me.

On one occasion, an evangelical guard was sent to watch us. "Yes, Saúl, I am also a member of this family of faith," he said.

Periodically this guard would fix it so that he could come to our cellblock. He let us come out of our cells and would share the Word of God with us. He also comforted us and encouraged us in a great way.

In addition, the Lord allowed us to produce a bulletin of news and meditations, with a number of different sections. It also included crossword puzzles with biblical themes. I greatly enjoyed doing all of this.

We had also started up a library with evangelical material, and the group of brothers continued to grow.

At the same time, however, it was very painful for me not to be able to touch or embrace my mother. I had been in the habit of showing her great affection and caring.

Despite this, she comforted me with words full of significance. "Hold fast to the Lord. Put your faith in him. Hopefully I will soon have you at my side again."

And, in faith, I said, "Don't worry, Mum; very soon God will do what is right."

My case was extremely difficult. The Christian lawyers were very honest in their efforts to explain the difficulties to me. I understood.

After they had sentenced me to 20 years in prison I had become very unconcerned about the whole trial process. Fortunately I have a family who are full of love for me, and they remained constantly concerned about my freedom.

The brothers and sisters at Peace and Hope kept looking for ways to obtain my freedom. Until 1996, however, there didn't seem to be any legal recourse in my case. There were a large number of anomalies in my trial. The first problem was that I did not actually have rights to any kind of recourse, because I had been sentenced and the sentence had been confirmed, but, at the same time, I had not received a fair trial. My witness statement did not contain one word that had come from my own mouth. I had not been allowed to say a thing in my own defence.

My hope was reawakened when the Ad Hoc Commission for Pardons was formed. The norms and rules of this Commission seemed adequate for my situation.

The Christian lawyers prepared my file and presented it to the Commission. I had my first interview after one month.

Everything that the Commission lawyer asked me was exactly what I had wished that the original judges had asked me before they sentenced me. It was a fluent dialogue. There were no contradictions; I responded to each question with the simple truth.

During that period I was not allowed to leave my cell, but the lawyer German Vargas regularly came to see me. I was interviewed three times in over one month. The last interview lasted almost two hours. The Commission lawyer was almost convinced of my innocence, but I told him that, if he decided I should stay in prison, that would be all right.

"I now have work in the prison, alongside the other Christians," I told him.

"Ah! You're an evangelical!"

Almost immediately he took me into another room and introduced me to two Catholic nuns. They said a few things to me and asked me a few uncomfortable questions. It became a bit of an ideological confrontation. I answered in a cordial and loving spirit because the Word of God wasn't given to us for us to fight over.

It seemed that the lawyer had wanted us to face each other. He thought that I would become violent, or something along those lines.

One of the nuns caught on to this apparent scheme of his and asked the lawyer, "Why are you doing this to this boy? He has worked with me for years in the area of health in the prison."

It was true; I knew her well!

After the final interview German returned to visit me. I told him everything and began to cry. Everything was in God's hands.

That same day, my mother visited me, as she did every month. I gave her a few of my things. "Take them back to the house!" I said.

I wanted to believe that I would be set free. Throughout that period I would wake up each morning hoping to hear good news.

One week later, on 29th October 1997, a friend, Juan Cruces, was handing out the daily rations and, upon arriving at my cell, he said, "You're leaving. I heard your name on the radio." And he happily went on his way.

Just then, many others came over to congratulate me. Someone brought a radio and tuned it to a Peruvian radio programme. I believed them, but I needed to hear my name for myself.

There was a newsflash and the voice of the journalist Guido Lombardi said, "List of those pardoned: Saúl Tito Coicca . . ."

At that moment so many things flashed through my mind: university, my family, my degree . . .

Everyone congratulated me. I hid myself for a moment and cried by myself. There were so many thoughts flooding my mind.

At approximately 8:00 or 9:00 in the morning a policeman came to tell me that it was time to go. Half an hour later he arrived at my cell with some documents, opened up the cell and let me out. Immediately I began to give away my personal items to those who needed them, my sandals and my shoes, etc – I didn't want to take anything away with me, except for my Bible and my English book.

I apportioned responsibilities to the group of brothers whom I was leaving behind and said my goodbyes. We touched hands through the bars, as they sang my favourite hymns. I couldn't leave. My feet were heavy. I felt as though I were leaving my family behind. They were feelings similar to those I had experienced when I first came to prison. Only, this time, it was a new family.

At the door, German was happily waiting for me. My family

were outside the prison waiting for me. Representatives of other organisations were also there to be with those they had defended. Two hours later, Father Hubert Lanssiers, a member of the Ad Hoc Commission, arrived with the official proof of our pardons. After a long wait, we were finally able to leave at 5:00 in the afternoon. There were five of us who got out that day.

At first as I left the prison I could not make out my family. My nearsightedness had worsened in prison and I had difficulties seeing clearly. My heart burned with the desire to embrace them, but I could not see them. We had walked down two streets when I suddenly spotted a cloud of dust coming quickly towards me. My anxiety blinded me even further until finally . . . my little sister threw herself into my arms. Behind her, I could make out my mother and my father. So much time had gone by. The pain showed in their faces and bodies; they looked older. We embraced and wept uncontrollably.

That night, various friends came to visit me. Some of the brothers and sisters from church came, along with the pastor. A number of relatives arrived. The day that God returned my freedom to me was full of so many emotions. Today, my entire family are evangelicals and each day I feel stronger.

### Notes

1   A centre of preparation for university.
2   The founder of the Shining Path, who would have been recognised by any Peruvian.
3   Yanamayo prison is located in Puno in south-eastern Peru. Because of the extreme cold and the high altitude it is well known for being one of the worst prisons in all of Peru.

# CHAPTER SIX

# WUILLE

After the armed forces took over the state universities in Peru in May 1991, many students, professors and other staff workers became the subject of investigations and were later accused of subversive activity. The invasion by the armed forces took place at all of the national universities, contravening the law of university autonomy.

Two universities, the National University of San Marcos and the Enrique Guzman and Valle University, also known as La Cantuta, were singled out as "hubs of subversive activity". The one thing that these institutions had in common was that the majority of their student populations came from both the provinces and the lower socio-economic levels of Peruvian society.

Wuille Ruiz Figueroa studied at both of these universities. He began to study economics at San Marcos University in 1979, but was able to finish only one year of study because of continual strikes by the professors and service personnel. Dissatisfied with the development of his classes at San Marcos, and out of a desire to learn more about judicial development and Peruvian politics, he began to study law at the Federico Villarreal University in 1982.

That same year, at the age of 23, Wuille also took up formal membership of the Methodist Church of Peru. He had had his initial conversion experience at the age of fifteen during a retreat in the city of Chosica, and prior to that he had attended Sunday school at the San Martín de Porres Methodist Church, along with his four brothers and one sister.

As a youth, Wuille had always been an eager participant in church activities, and was a member of the primary, secondary and youth leagues. Later, when he took up his official church membership he became a delegate to the District Assembly, representing his local youth movement. He was also the president of the directors' committee at his local church.

His next move was to the district of San Miguel in Lima, where he attended the Methodist Church in Miramar. He later returned to San Martín and began studying anew at San Marcos, where he enrolled in two professional degree courses. His studies, along with work and other activities, took him away somewhat from his church activities.

While at San Marcos University he became interested in politics, and decided to take part in the elections for the federal centre in his department. At the same time he also joined in a range of other student activities, where he met people with a variety of different political opinions.[1]

He finished his economics studies in 1988, and received his Bachelor's degree from San Marcos University. Two years later he obtained a Bachelor of Law degree from Villarreal University. By this time he had also married his wife, Silvia, another economist, whom he met at San Marcos. In 1992 their daughter Estelí was born.

While he was finishing his studies Wuille began to work at a variety of jobs. He washed cars for a Chrysler contractor; he worked as a bricklayer, a bookseller and a salesman of household utensils; he worked as a caretaker in businesses and factories, and he also helped give mathematics classes.

In 1990 when he finished his law degree, he was given a placement at CENTROMIN-Peru, a state-owned mining company. This meant he had to travel to La Oroya in the Andean highlands. At the end of that year there was a call for participants in another placement at a non-profit drug-prevention centre, called CEDRO. Wuille was given a place and began working at the centre the following year.

Wuille first began visiting the prisons in Lima while working with the drug-prevention programme. He was still working at CEDRO when the police arrested him on 25th February 1993. After five years of wrongful imprisonment, Wuille left the Castro Castro Prison on 6th June 1998.

After his release, Peace and Hope opened its doors to Wuille to help him generate some initial income. His efforts to provide for his family were hampered, however, as he waited for the return of his personal documents and the annulment of his prison record.

Because many Christians outside Peru took an interest in the human-rights situation there, Wuille was invited on a number of occasions to speak in European countries including Scotland, England, Holland and Germany, as well as in California.

His stay in prison left him with a number of holes in his life, which he is filling by being reunited with his family and by working with the Bernabe Group, a Christian community of evangelical ex-prisoners.

Wuille gives the following testimony, detailing his stay in prison, his sorrows and his joys.

# I

I was detained on the night of 25th February 1993. The police arrived at my home at 9:30, saying that they were carrying out a registration of the inhabitants. My wife and my ten-month-old daughter were in the house with me.

There were about ten or twelve heavily armed policemen. I let them in; they came inside and began to question me as they examined every corner of the house. They looked on the roof, near the walls, at the floor, the furniture, the beds, clothes, books, notebooks – everything was suspicious to them.

At the time I worked at the CEDRO Institute (the Centre for Information and Education to Prevent the use of Drugs), in a drug-prevention programme in the San Jorge Men's Prison and the Chorrillos Women's Prison. In addition, my work involved coordinating the work of other Christian institutions such as the National Evangelical Council of Peru (CONEP) and the Episcopal Commission for Social Action (CEAS). These two institutions attended to the various needs of the prisoners by doing pastoral, social and legal work. My work also involved some cooperation with the National Penitentiary Institute (INPE).

The police began to ask me a series of questions: where I worked, what I did, how much I earned, etc. Afterwards, they started to make a series of accusations against me: that I was a terrorist, that I had taken part in the kidnapping and death of a businessman, that I was in charge of the terrorists' finances. They wanted to know where I had studied, why I had been able to travel outside Peru, if I knew how to use guns or explosives, etc. They pushed me against the wall and took my wife into another room to interrogate her separately.

The house was catalogued bit by bit. At the end, at about 1:00 in the morning, they took me out of the house. Before they took me away my wife asked them to let me say good-bye to my little daughter, who had slept through the whole thing. Perhaps she was dreaming that the next day she would see her father and he would help her to take her first steps. It was only two months before her first birthday.

I had been wrongly accused of collaborating with terrorists, because of a certain person whom I had known at San Marcos University when I was studying economics, who was a student leader there. This person had asked me to look after some documents, which unknown to me turned out to contain subversive material. Because of this, the policemen laid the blame on me and told me that I should have denounced that person as a terrorist.

They took me to the National Anti-Terrorism Directorate (DINCOTE) for fifteen days. During this period I talked to a lawyer, who seemed to find it hard to give me adequate legal aid. I was incommunicado to my family – I was able to see them only for one day before they transferred me to the Public Ministry. The day after my arrest they made me sign an Act of Detention, which was not in accordance with the correct procedure, because the public prosecutor wasn't present. They threatened me with torture and said they would arrest my wife if I didn't sign it.

Spending the night in DINCOTE is like staying in a castle of terror. Men and women are taken out of their cells after midnight, a dark hour when lawyers, public prosecutors and human-rights representatives do not exist. This is an hour of macabre clamour, of confusing noises, beatings, cries of fright and pain and deep sighs that are lost among the cold and dismal cell walls. They were the cries of the prisoners, the broken images of God, who were being tortured.

Those cries stuck in my head; they hammered at my ears and kept me from sleeping. Those cries informed us that the

next victim could be one of us. I thought that at any moment
the policemen might just give a wave of the hand, as they did
on many occasions, and it would be "goodbye, life". At times
like that, when one feels as though one's physical integrity is
in danger, it can seem as though anything could happen.

All of those cries became like a "curtain of music". It was a
rhythm that moved, almost like a salsa at high volume. All of
a sudden the police would try to silence the grating shouts,
and the message was, "Cooperate or this could happen to
you."

As night fell, rats invaded the prison. They roamed around
at their ease, and visited us cell by cell. Sniffing, they climbed
over our bodies. They shrieked and fought amongst themselves over a prisoner or some rubbish.

Who is ever prepared to be detained? In prison, your principles are questioned down to every last detail. When I arrived
at DINCOTE I had an uncontrollable need to relieve myself,
but I had nothing with which to clean myself. In my desperation I saw a bit of dirty toilet paper and, losing every bit of
pride, I took it and used it. The instinct to survive in prison
directs how one copes with situations like this.

We were forced to stay shut up for 24 hours in those tiny
cells. They would take us out in groups of ten for only fifteen
minutes to empty our bowels. There were no toilets on which
to sit. We had to defecate in the urinals, all ten of us at the
same time, just as a group right before us had done, and so the
filth built up.

On the rare occasion that there was some water, the police
would rush us through just to find that it had run out when it
got to our turn. When this happened the rats would come out
of their holes as if they were laughing spectators at some kind
of tragi-comedy. We turned the handle and nothing came out;
nothing from the shower either. What was I supposed to do

after they had brought me here without soap, without a tooth-brush, with no towel, no change of clothes, no pyjamas?

A few moments before arriving in DINCOTE they had covered my head with a sweater, and made me duck down and go down some stairs while they held on to my hands. Bit by bit I began to hear the sound of heartbreaking cries and plead-ing mixed with threatening shouts and blatant lies. They were asking them to reveal names and dates about different people and deeds. Those are shouts that even now that I am free I continue to hear. They resound in my mind and force me to cry out for the observance of the minimum rules for the treat-ment of prisoners.

I arrived in DINCOTE at about 2:30 in the morning. That night they took me into a cell where there were already three other people, who gave me a welcome of sorts. One of them had been there for 30 days, another for ten. When I heard this it seemed like an eternity to me, but I was sure that my legal situation would be resolved the next day. I spent that night awake, being interrogated, thinking of my family and killing the fleas that little by little seemed to be eating me away.

Later that night the interrogator arrived. He took me out of the cell and a policeman came to ask me a series of questions. After a while another would come and ask me the same ques-tions. Some of them threatened me; others tried to build up a level of confidence, calling me "friend" and telling me that if I cooperated they could apply the "repentance law", and that way I could leave the prison the next day with a new identity for me and my family and we could go and live in a foreign country, with money. After five days they made me sign another act of detention and began to threaten me all over again.

"You don't want us to arrest your wife, do you?"

"There won't be a public prosecutor or an attorney; then what will you be able to do?"

That same afternoon, when it was our turn to go to the bathroom and everyone was desperate to urinate or wash themselves, the police, perhaps because they were in a bad mood or because they simply did not feel like it, refused to open our cells. In desperation and with bursting bladders, we began to shout and bang on the bars. In a while another policeman, with more authority, came to quieten everyone down. After we had explained to him what had happened, he allowed us to go out. Afterwards, that same policeman began to preach to us about Jesus Christ and the message of salvation.

A few days after I was imprisoned a young boy of only 17 years of age was killed. He was nicknamed "boa" because he came from the jungle region. The boy had been hit in the head by a bullet when one of the policemen's guns had discharged. We heard only the sound of the shot, a quiet moan, and then the dry thump of a lifeless body falling to the floor. This happened very close to our cell and, although we didn't see it, we heard what happened very clearly. Later we walked past the place where the boy had fallen. There was an immense puddle of blood already coagulated, and around it the chalk marks outlining the place where the body had been. I do not think that even this event had much of an effect on the overall condition and treatment of prisoners, because he was only a "supposed terrorist", or perhaps it was because he didn't have any family who lived in the area to protest on his behalf.

In the end, I was accused of being a "terrorist collaborator". Leaving DINCOTE was like regaining the confidence that one needs to go on living, almost as if life had been returned to me. I had a rash of injuries all over my body and it itched incessantly – especially between my legs. I had lost a few kilos. I was caged up with other prisoners as we were transported to the Justice Palace. The people that drove by stared at us –

some in disgust, others in commiseration. But of course the judgement didn't rest with them.

The little prison in the Justice Palace became another sort of crossroads. I waited there in the basement for three more months. Someone once said that that building is too big for so little justice. My stay there was like that of a rat in a sewer: no natural light, intense humidity, blocked-up toilets and, nauseatingly, human waste all over the place. The urinals overflowed onto the floor because the drainage system was insufficient. We were forced to share cells with common criminals – accused of robbery, murder and rape. The employees of INPE treated us as though we were worthless and humiliated both us and our families, who were forced to wait in long queues just to bring us food to eat. Even then, the families were obliged to pay an under-the-table fee just to see us – or even just to find out if we were still alive.

## II

On 18th June 1993 I was transferred to the Castro Castro Maximum Security Prison. I lived a life there that was not much different from before. Three of us slept in each cell, which measured two metres by three metres. Because there were only cement beds for two, one person had to sleep on the floor. There was a hole inside the cell for us to take care of our bodily needs. There was a tap where, from time to time, a little water came out. There were also periods when no water came out for days at a time and we had to either use water that we had hoarded or be taken to other places that were reached by going down ladders. On one of these occasions I developed a lesion on my back. This lesion got worse and worse from sleeping on a cement bed with only a very thin sponge mattress for over five years. When there was no water the cell gave off a putrid odour. There was no way in which to clean the hole in which we had to relieve ourselves, bathe and wash clothes.

Living with two other men in such close confinement was like being in a forced marriage. If there are sometimes problems between a couple who love each other, one can imagine what can happen between three people who spend 23½ hours every day shut up together with only half an hour to enjoy fresh air on the patio. In those circumstances, however, even the air itself felt as if it were a prisoner too.

After being imprisoned for a while some of us formed a group that identified with the Christian faith. Little by little the Lord gave us demonstrations of his presence with us in the midst of the pain and the desperation. We felt that he was with us and that he, too, was suffering with us. These cells, which at first had seemed like tombs, now began to praise the name of God and to preach the Word. At the beginning it had seemed insane to be shut up in the worst of conditions and yet to continue to praise God. The other prisoners, who lived by violence, suspected that we were spies, infiltrators, or "repented" terrorists because we distanced ourselves from them and did not share their attitudes.

Because of security regulations we were not allowed to have notebooks or writing utensils or any kind of hidden reading material. If we managed to find an opportunity to write anything we had to be very careful so that our words could not be misinterpreted by the police. They read every letter that came out of our cells.

Throughout 1993 and part of 1994 pastoral workers were not allowed into our cellblocks. All direct contact with prisoners was prohibited. However, some Christians came to the prisons anyway. They were like real angels sent by the Lord to visit the lepers of our age, those that humanity had rejected and sent away from society in an effort to avoid chaos and public disorder.

In 1994 we formed a "prayer workshop" with a group of Evangelical and Catholic brothers. We put aside our theological differences and made the most of every opportunity to meet together in our cells to pray and read the Bible. We meditated together and looked for ways to tell others about the Lord.

The cells were cold and damp. The draught that came in through the slits in the walls lowered the temperature even more. In the winter we felt as though we were caged in iceboxes as the cold battered our muscles and penetrated our bones. The hills that surrounded the prison were silent witnesses to this suffering. In addition, the work detail to which I was assigned meant I was in contact with water in the middle of winter. This deeply affected my muscles and circulation.

I also remember that once, during a football game, I was hit in the leg, which then swelled up enormously. Faced with a negative and indifferent attitude from the police guards I wound up having to give myself an injection.

I also felt that my vision was worsening. There was no electric light in the cell, only in the corridors. At night a little bit of opaque light would filter in, fragmented into numerous parallel lines, which we had to take advantage of in order to continue reading.

The year after I was arrested my mother died. On 31st December 1993 she had an accident in the house. She endured fourteen days of agony. I remember that on 14th January 1994 I woke up suddenly before dawn. I had been dreaming about my mother. I dreamt we were travelling to Huanta, Ayacucho, her native city, when all of a sudden a dead relative of ours appeared. He raised his hand in joy at our arrival, which frightened me, and I woke up thinking how strange it was to be greeted by a relative who had been dead for years. I told my mother all of this in a letter I was writing to her that day, as the fourteenth was also the day of the monthly visit to the prisons. In the same letter I also promised my mother that one of the first things I would do when I was released from prison would be to obtain my lawyer's qualification. This was an unusual thing for me to do because I didn't usually like making promises.

My mother had just passed away. My wife told me this in the final ten minutes of the allocated half-hour that we had to see each other. It was a terrible shock, to know that I would never see her again, that I would not be able to say goodbye to her. I tried to lift myself above it all, to remain serene, because my mother was like that, always a serene woman. I looked at her photo, which my wife had brought for me. I began to hum songs; I had no appetite to eat anything. The other men expressed their condolences to me, but only the individual can understand the depth of his or her own pain. At about two o'clock in the morning I woke up in floods of tears that I was unable to contain.

I thought back to the ceremony marking the culmination of my law studies in the Lawyers' College of Lima in 1990. I remembered how my mother had helped me put on my robes. It was actually she who should have been graduating, not me. I believe that my mother probably bartered her life for my freedom.

My mother also had a deep love for Mexico – she knew a little about the country's environment, customs and geography from movies she had seen, and thought that it closely resembled Ayacucho, her birthplace.

After that I felt that death was all around me. Once I began to understand the unforeseeable things that can happen inside a prison I realised that it was possible that I might never return home. Sometimes I imagined that they took me out of the prison wrapped up in a blanket and that they threw my lifeless body onto a pile of others, like a mound of potatoes. These feelings grew even stronger when I received news of other relatives or friends who had also passed away.

One of these friends was Arturo Encarnación Nieto, a law student, who was considered by Amnesty International to be a prisoner of conscience. He was defended by a number of human-rights organisations but died in prison in 1995, delirious and exhibiting other signs of dementia. He became totally debilitated after an extremely painful ordeal. His death actually took place while his case was being reviewed for the second time in the courts. His first trial had been before "faceless judges" and he was sentenced to 20 years. We later discovered that he had been declared innocent, but by that time Arturo had already died. He died in prison an innocent man.

One year after my mother died, my wife's mother also passed away – another blow for her and for me. Who else was going to join that ill-fated list?

Family visits were actually one of the cruellest and most sophisticated forms of psychological torture, for both the prisoners and the families themselves. Only two immediate family members were allowed to visit at a time – a parent, wife, son or daughter. If the prisoner only had cousins, aunts and uncles, family that lived at a distance, or relatives who couldn't prove their kinship, that prisoner would remain alone and forsaken, because the police would not authorise a visitor's card.

Visits took place only once a month. These days were among the most nerve-wracking for the prisoners. We were given just 30 minutes. We were not allowed to embrace our visitor, and were unable even to touch their hand because there were metal sheets and bars between us that prevented us from doing so. We could just make out our visitor through a grille – a broken image of a thousand pieces, like a puzzle. We felt a huge impotence at seeing our family members crying on the other side of the grille, and they probably also felt sad and angry at having to see us in such a rush, as if they were visiting the zoo.

Children who were not of legal age were only allowed to visit every three months. The authorities wanted to destroy our capacity to love, dehumanising us and breaking the bonds between the prisoner and their family. In many cases they were successful, because after so many years in prison and in the face of a difficult economic situation family unity was affected and often finally broke under the strain. My little daughter, whom I had left at ten months of age, didn't call me "Daddy" any more; she only guessed that maybe I was her "uncle".

In prison, one of my favourite occupations was reading. This opened up a way for me to begin writing some narratives, poems, newsletters and testimonies about my time in prison. At the end of 1994, a prison library was created. There, shut up in my cell in the half-light, I was able to read and give free rein to fantasy. I began to familiarise myself with the works of many national and international authors whom I had never before had the opportunity to enjoy. I went on to read the letters of the Apostle Paul in prison, the Cuban Valladares, the Frenchman Belbenaut and the Argentine Timmermann and Isabel Allende of Chile – all of which affected me deeply, motivating me to write my own story in order to tell about the world in which I was living.

Little by little I began to understand more about the messages of Job and the Psalms and of other various Bible passages that one sometimes reads lightly or skips over unperceived. I went on to rediscover the experiences of Paul, Peter and Jesus himself in prison, as they were all unjustly condemned.

I began to receive thousands of letters from many different countries: Holland, the USA, France, Switzerland, England and Germany, etc – as well as South Africa, China and Singapore! All of these had a message for the brothers in prison: "God does not abandon his sons. We are praying for you, your family and for all the prisoners. The Lord will strengthen you and he will give you freedom." The prison permitted only some of these letters to enter, but now that I am in freedom I can hold and look at the thousands of letters, with beautiful drawings from children, which arrived from many different countries around the world.

## III

The "faceless judges" condemned me to 20 years in prison, which meant that I would not be released until 2013. Dr Regalado had put together a masterly defence but his arguments were not taken into account and what's more, the "faceless judges" hadn't even *considered* taking them into account. The sentence was read out only fifteen minutes after the lawyer put forward his defence.

But one is stubborn and puts one's hope in justice – even when things turn out this way. Because real justice is God – this justice that one seems to receive as if one were in front of an immense sea, feeling the soft afternoon breeze and watching the rolling of the waves, and in which one discovers a resplendent sun that bathes the waters, forming a multi-coloured sky. This is how justice should be – a type of mantle that covers all the earth with its immense and brilliant sunlight.

On 28th July 1996, in his message to the nation, Alberto Fujimori admitted that judicial errors had been made in the terrorism trials. The Ad Hoc Commission was created, consisting of the Ombudsman, Dr Santisteban, the Minister of Justice, and the priest Father Hubert Lanssiers. This Commission began to evaluate individual cases. They would then make recommendations to President Fujimori regarding applications for pardon and the right of grace that would allow him to free any innocent prisoners. This whole process took place thanks to God and was the result of three things: the vigorous efforts of many human-rights organisations, both in Peru and abroad; the work of the church, which maintained its commitment to justice, and the heroic and relentless efforts of the family members of the prisoners, who persistently knocked on the closed doors of justice regardless of the fact that it had always seemed completely inaccessible to the poor and the marginalised.

The Commission's technical secretary carried out a fairly professional job that permitted a spark of hope, which had almost gone out, to be revived.

Some of the prison conditions improved after 1997. These changes mainly affected those who were in prison on terrorism-related charges but who had later been classified by the prison authorities as being of minimum risk. The visiting room was done away with and visits were now direct, weekly, and much longer. The food also got notably better and now occupational courses were implemented and taught by teachers from the Ministry of Education in a cooperation agreement with INPE. Conjugal visits, however, were still not permitted, above all for those who remained in the medium- and maximum-security cellblocks.

The creation of "pilot cellblocks" in 1995 was a very important factor in the betterment of prison conditions and it became a channel for alternative ways of regaining one's freedom. In those cellblocks one could find innocent prisoners without any ties to terrorism, but in addition to them one would also find other men and women who at some point in their lives had chosen violence as a means of resolving the country's problems but who had later renounced those links and dedicated themselves to the road of reconciliation and the reconstruction of life, peace and justice. Many of them had accepted the gospel in a new birth while in prison. The Christian communities inside those cellblocks looked for ways of creating new alternative spaces for living in the Christian faith, although this way was not always free from error.

There are still innocent men and women in prison. I strongly believe that, together with the cases of the innocent and the "repented", the cases of those who have broken off ties with the terrorist movements should also be considered for early release. The authorities should consider reducing their sentences and implementing prison benefits, such as earning credit on their sentence for work and study, semi-freedom and conditional liberty.

I would like to conclude this testimony by thanking God for keeping his promise to set the captives free, and for so many gestures of prayer and solidarity. Thanks too to the human-rights institutions, both the Evangelical and the Catholic Churches that are committed to justice, especially the Evangelical Association of Peace and Hope and the National Evangelical Council of Peru (CONEP); the pastoral agents, Madeleine, Ned, Elena, Edy; the Agape Network of Open Doors, Christian Solidarity, Mission to the East in Holland, The Committee for Solidarity and Human Rights between Europe and Peru in Germany; CEDRO; journalists like Tito Perez from "The Truth"; CEPS; to FEDEPAZ; the Episcopal Commission for Social Action (CEAS); Congressman Abanto; my friends Janet, Elvia, Oscar, Liliana, Quique, Jimena, Eduardo and Rodolfo – so many people and so many institutions that it would take far too long to name them all. To my family, Silvia and Estelí, who knew how to hope and how to recover. To Flavia, Hugo, Juan and Walter. To all those who prayed for the prisoners and continue to do so – and also to those who did not – may God bless you.

## IV

In August 1998, two months after leaving prison, I had the privilege of starting to work with Peace and Hope, the same institution that the Lord had used to regain my freedom. At the beginning, my work dealt mostly with social support for prisoners and their families. That same year, I had to go back to the prison where I had lived for more than five years. This visit to the prison was highly emotional for me and it filled me with sadness to see so many of our brothers still imprisoned. It seemed incredible to me to be back there as a visitor while they, months later, were still prisoners. As I left the prison I could not hide a sudden fear that one of the guards, whom I had known inside, might classify me as one of the prisoners and even give the order not to let me leave – but this was just a passing impression.

After I was freed, one of my main goals was to obtain my qualification as a lawyer at university so that I could join the Lima College of Lawyers. This was the promise that I had made my mother in the letter I wrote to her on the day of her death in 1994. To achieve this, I had to go over various hurdles, one of which, namely getting my criminal record expunged, took a number of months. Finally, at the end of 1998, a specific law was issued that allowed this to take place. After that was done I resubmitted my transcripts to the university. It seems that the Lord had all of his timing planned, because only ten days before going to Europe at the invitation of Open Doors and Christian Solidarity Worldwide, on the final day of March 1999, I was able to take my much-longed-for final exam, which I passed with a good grade.

In October of that year I received my title as a lawyer and began to work in legal defence, specifically on the cases that Peace and Hope were defending. I took part in a number of cases before different state entities, including the Ombudsman, the Ministry of Justice and the Public Ministry, mostly concerned with the situation of wrongfully imprisoned men and women. Since that date I have not stopped reading documents, going before judicial tribunals, interviewing men and women in prison, visiting other cities and prisons in Peru, and speaking with the families of the prisoners, all of whom live in impoverished conditions but who maintain one hope – to see their loved ones free again.

I also remember having to return to DINCOTE, the same place where I passed the worst fifteen days of my life. This time it was to investigate the cases of some Christians who had been detained. As I walked back into those same surroundings, going up and down the stairs and speaking with the policemen who worked there, my experiences came flooding back to my memory. The cries of those who were terribly mistreated and tortured; the audible impact of the bullet crashing through a young boy's body; the questioning and requestioning spewed out like darts alongside insults and blows; the rats that kept us company during the long nights, encouraging us with their squeaking and stealing our crusts of bread; the nauseating cells; the cries of hope and justice that fought not to be extinguished.

In December 2001, when I was instrumental in regaining freedom for Juana Lazo Ramirez and her husband, Victor Maco Navarte, I truly felt that God had acted with justice and mercy. When this happened, I felt profoundly moved to have been able to contribute to the liberation of a husband and wife, reunited in freedom after almost nine years in separate prisons. This seemed incredible to me, and for this reason I told the Lord that now he could take me away with him. I felt like a tiny tool and I put my profession in his hands. Each time that I go before the judicial tribunals or before the authorities in charge of deciding a request for freedom, I understand more and more how small we are in the larger scheme of things. I see how the Lord directs things, so I always ask him to do his will. Once I was given the case of three impoverished peasant men from Ayacucho. I defended the case before the Pardoning Commission at the Ministry of Justice – two of the men were condemned to life in prison and the third was condemned to 30 years in prison – I was accompanied by Dee Daniels, a Christian lawyer from the USA who was doing an internship at Peace and Hope. We entered the Ministry of Justice together and she committed herself to pray for me as I argued the cases of the three innocent men. After a few minutes, I was told that the Commission had decided to approve pardons for all three men – the Lord spoke and acted simultaneously.

My work as a lawyer also gave me the opportunity to meet the mother of Julio Cusihuaman, "la Mama Candy". She was only able to communicate in Quechua. I tried to empathise with her sadness for her son in prison. Two Christian Solidarity Worldwide representatives, Anna Lee and Neil Dixe, also met her at the beginning of the year 2000. We climbed up to her humble home at the top of a hill and she invited us to eat tuna (or prickly pear cactus), a popular Andean fruit in Peru, from her garden. I saw my own mother as I watched her; she was also Quechua-speaking and it was her memory that gave me the strength to become someone who sought some justice. One night in Lima we had a prayer meeting for the work of Peace and Hope. One of the Christian women who came that night asked us to pray for Julio's

freedom – they were from the same church; this also motivated me even more and, finally, Julio is now also a free man
thanks to the power of God.

From these heights, after four years of working as a lawyer,
I should renew my thanks for having been given the opportunity to know the Christians at Peace and Hope – the institution that welcomed me and gave me a helping hand. To
German, Alfonso, Gloria, the two Ruths, the two Josés,
Loyda, Roger, Libia, Mitzi, Juancito, Lourdes – I believe that
the Lord shows himself through each of them. I also give
thanks for having had the opportunity to meet so many
Christians in Peru and in other countries, a list of their names
would be too long – institutions and countries; children, teenagers, adults and the elderly, people who on many occasions
could communicate with me only through signs – but I could
see reflected in their faces an intense happiness to see me
among them, someone whom they knew only through news
articles or photos.

The Lord has made me a very privileged person and,
although these five years of freedom have not been free from
burdens and obstacles, I am adamant and will go on repeat-
ing that it continues to be a privilege.

The situation in our country has made it difficult to defend
human rights, but despite this, however, we do now have a
Truth and Reconciliation Commission whose work it is to
uncover what happened during the internal conflict and to
generate processes for truth, justice and reconciliation among
all Peruvians. This is an effort in which Peace and Hope has
also maintained a presence as, during almost 20 years of conflict, many evangelical brothers and sisters were murdered,
others were forcibly "disappeared", others were tortured or
plucked from their homes. Now we should be seeing the
beginning of an understanding of why so much violence

occurred and where the bodies of those who were murdered are located. There should be investigations into what happened to the disappeared. At the same time, I still do not know what my life will finally be, nor the places or destinations to which the Lord will lead me. I hope to continue contributing by being a useful tool for the justice of God, resplendent in my heart; there is so much to do. I cannot boast of accumulating riches or material goods, in fact there are days when we only just scrape together enough money to pay for our daily requirements – but this is what it is to work in defence of human rights – not, as some wrongly believe, to become millionaires. In any case, we enrich ourselves with the satisfaction of serving others.

## Note

1   It was during this period that he met the person who, years later, asked him to hold on to an envelope full of documents that turned out to be subversive material. These were used as conclusive proof against Wuille. A few days before he received the envelope he had noticed the presence of strange people around his house.

# CHAPTER SEVEN

# JULIO

Julio was one of the prisoners defended by Wuille Ruiz Figueroa after his release. He tells his story below.

I was born on 15th July 1971 among the mountain peaks of Peru, in Chuschi, a small, poor village in the department of Ayacucho. My parents, like the majority of people in that area, had serious financial difficulties and suffered from alcoholism. Their marriage had produced two children, myself and my little sister. I was about three years old when Catalina, my sister, was born and we moved to Huamanga, the capital of Ayacucho. We settled in one of the poorest neighbourhoods, where, together with my parents and sister, I spent my childhood and adolescence.

When I had just turned eleven years old I received the first great emotional shock of my life, my father's death from alcoholism. After that point I became responsible for providing for my family, since my mother was also addicted to drink and never brought home any provisions for her children. I had only just finished primary school, where I had attended morning classes, but now things were different. I wanted to continue studying so I began attending night classes so that I could work during the day. I dreamed of becoming something very different from what my parents had become.

I was sixteen years old when Catalina died from a medical condition she had had since early childhood. This was extremely painful for me, because it was Catalina who had always encouraged me. Because of her illness she had been unable to attend school but at thirteen years old she already reasoned like a grown woman – and encouraged me to continue studying. After this, instead of getting better, my mother's drinking grew even worse and she would sometimes disappear for days and even weeks at a time.

Six months before I reached 20 I was just one month away from finishing my higher studies. I was studying for a technical degree in order to be a teacher's assistant in primary education. I was in the middle of my class and had been asked to read aloud, when all of a sudden a policeman dressed in civilian clothes burst into the classroom. He tricked me into coming outside with him so that no one would realise that he was a policeman, and on the way to the police station he began to hit me, telling me that I was a terrorist.

Inside the police station, however, things became even worse. It was there that I first experienced torture. This is impossible for me to describe with mere words. I remember that they began with shouts and threats and then they tied me up. They beat me all over my body, and when I lost consciousness they revived me with a bucket of icy water. They hit me over and over again with metal objects and with their guns and batons. They threw me against the wall and to the floor. They tied my hands behind my back with a thin rope and lifted me up off the floor by my wrists – and then hammered me with blows. They mercilessly plunged my head into a tub full of water and detergent, brutally choking me. Then the hour of electric shocks arrived. They applied them to my temples, eyebrows, cheeks, chest, fingers and toes and to my genitals. The most disgusting thing was when they pushed my head into a toilet full of human waste.

They never showed the smallest amount of compassion – even as I cried out, "Please, master – don't hit me; I don't know anything!" As I writhed on the floor, my cries of pain sounded more like the shrieks of some strange animal. The reply, like some sort of frightening, macabre music in the background, was always, "Say that you did it and we won't hit you any more and we won't kill you." This continued for about three hours every night for nine days – the same blows, the same threats, the same electric shocks – until my veins felt as though they would explode. They continued to make up the same stories – that I, as part of a terrorist network, had planted two car bombs in an attack on a police convoy, resulting in the death of eleven policemen, had murdered five civilians, had been promoting terrorist propaganda in "people's schools" and had painted graffiti with terrorist slogans.

I lived in Vista Alegre (Happy View), an area considered by the authorities to be a "Red Zone" – perhaps because of the poverty in which we all lived, or perhaps in order to explain the high murder rate. Many people were killed in my neighbourhood but we never knew whether the culprits were the police, the army or the terrorists. In addition to that, my birthplace, Chuschi, was where the terrorist activity had started, with the burning of the electoral ballot boxes in the 1980s. When all that was happening, however, I was just nine years old and living in Huamanga. However, now that I was detained, the facts that I had been born in Chuschi, lived in Vista Alegre and was studying in higher education were decisive proof that I was a terrorist – and the police wanted me to incriminate myself.

At about 5:00 one morning, after nine days had passed, one

of the other prisoners in the adjoining cell took pity on me and told me they were going to kill me that same afternoon. Later on, he said, the public prosecutor was coming to the prison and everyone except me was going to be taken down to the first floor, where it was easier to hear everyone's voices. As was his habit, the public prosecutor was going to ask if anyone had not been brought down, and the other prisoner told me I had to shout out at that point because that was my only hope.

Everything happened just as the prisoner had told me – if I had not cried out, the public prosecutor would never have known of my existence and I would have been killed. I was beaten for four more days as a punishment but then I was taken before the judges, who gave me unconditional liberty as they could find no proof of any terrorist involvement.

This whole experience traumatised me deeply, and out of fear I left Ayacucho and travelled to Lima. I was almost 20 years old, and although I had heard the gospel of Christ I had never accepted it because in my foolish reasoning there was no need.

In Lima I began to work in a market and, like my parents, using the little money that I earned I dedicated myself to drinking alcohol in order to forget the past. It was in the market that I met Vilma, a sensitive girl who was different from the other people that I knew. It turned out that she was a Christian. She quickly invited me to church and the third time I went along with her I accepted Christ as my Saviour. I didn't know what had happened but a very very great peace came over my heart and I forgot my bitterness and resentment and even my hatred towards the policemen who had tortured me.

In 1992, on 20th March, Vilma and I were married and the Lord began to bless us. I began to pray for my mother and that is how my mother, a life-long alcoholic, also came to the Lord and permanently ceased to drink. This was something that I could only attribute to the miracles of our Lord Jesus Christ. I began to grow in my faith – and started to study theology in my church. The church then commissioned me to start a church in my own home. We were later able to give it its own building, though we spent a great deal of time on our knees in order to do so – we built it to the glory of the Lord.

The Lord also began to teach me new things about himself by allowing me to pass through some very difficult experiences. In August 1998 my second son died of leukaemia after eleven months in hospital. Both the church in Vitarte and the church near my house gathered round to pray for me. There was one verse from God's Word that stayed in my head, which says, "Rest in my grace because in my strength your weakness will be made perfect" – so I just continued to say "Amen" to God in everything. Paul said that the Lord had prepared him for everything so that he might live life in abundance, and that for all those who love God everything works together for good, and this made me think of Joseph, the son of Jacob, who by the great hand of God was sent to Egypt in order to preserve the life of the entire tribe of Israel.

It was the beginning of January, 1999. Four months had passed since the death of Geraldo, my second son, and we were left with huge debts and very little business. Because of this I started to travel, selling razors and brushes in the provinces.

While travelling between two provincial cities, I was detained at one of the highway checkpoints and told that I was wanted for terrorist activity stemming from the original case of eight years ago. The checkpoint was in Oroya, one of the coldest places in Peru – I almost died because of the intense cold that night but the Lord had mercy on me and the next day I was transferred to Huancayo.

Vilma and my two children arrived and we cried out to the Lord, giving thanks for all the times he had responded to our prayers. We asked him for his will to be done with me and my family. After seven days there, which I used to preach the gospel, I was transferred to Ayacucho, where I continued to preach. The brothers and sisters from my church began to pray for me and sent letters to encourage me. I don't know how they did it but they contacted Peace and Hope, where the brothers and sisters began to work as my lawyers.

After only two months, however, I was sentenced to fifteen years in prison. I was unable to explain what had happened to me and those prisoners who were enemies of Christ began to mock my faith. I asked God, "Why?"

I then had a dream in which I saw myself building a house. I didn't understand this and I suffered greatly from being separated from my children and my wife, but the Lord takes care of the birds and I knew he would also take care of me and my family. I didn't know what else I should do then, but I began to speak about Christ and that is how we started the church inside the Maximum Security Prison of Yanamilla. As the other prisoners heard the message we began to grow in number little by little, until we numbered about 100 men. Many men experienced real freedom inside that prison because they now had Christ in their hearts. Of course, there were also many bitter and sad moments, when other prisoners and even some of the guards united themselves against me because of my faith to the point that I said, "Enough, Lord!"

But, through his love, many cards and letters began to arrive for me via the offices of Peace and Hope. At the beginning I thought it was very strange, because many of them were in English, but the brothers from Peace and Hope explained to me that these were from other brothers and sisters in Christ who had received news about me from Christian Solidarity Worldwide. They put this news out to other believers and now these people were praying for me and for my freedom. This filled me with a great strength in my spirit and I did not cease to tell the other prisoners about Christ because I was very sure that it was my God who was moving in all the hearts around the world.

I believe that God used me in the same way that he used Joseph. He put me there in order to save his children in that prison and to build a church that even now continues to be one of the strongest prison churches in all of Peru.

In the month of October, after 22 months of imprisonment, I was granted my freedom, but as I left my heart was very pained to leave so many of my sons in the faith behind. When I saw them weeping, from the oldest man to the youngest, I cried along with them as they embraced me and I reaffirmed my promise to them that I would continue to serve them even though I was permitted to leave this place. I departed on the twelfth of the month. Since then I have continued to visit the prisons in Peru – I would love to visit all of them but there are many things that limit me in my ability to do this.

Once I was free I returned to my house, but even my children didn't recognise me. Everything that we had had together was just a memory to them. We had lost everything – even the adobe house where we had lived had begun to fall apart because of the mist that falls in Lima. Water from a flood had also penetrated inside the house and everything inside was ruined – clothes, the bed, everything. We realised that it would be impossible for us to pay our debts in the situation in which we found ourselves. My wife and children became ill, and then I too became ill. We began to pray with even more persistence – up to now we had always seen the powerful hand of God move, and although at this point we could not see anything, in faith I began to work, visiting prisons with the support of the prayers of the church in Vitarte and of my wife. This was how I was appointed to be in charge of the prison ministry.

Peruvian churches are for the most part very impoverished, but they are rich in prayer. Throughout my schedule of visiting prisons, two or three weeks before each visit I would never have the money for the journeys, but this was always where the hand of God manifested itself. He always provided what was necessary for my trip. This is how I managed to arrive at the prisons of Chiclayo, Cajamarca, Huancayo, Ayacucho and the prisons in Lima. And I continue to travel to visit them. I would like to visit all of the prisons in Peru but of course I am limited because I also have to provide for my family.

All that I have done, however, I do voluntarily, out of gratitude to the Lord, because it is he who has paid the debts that I was unable to repay; he healed my pain and the pain of my family; he put peace in the hearts of all of my loved ones, and for the love of the prisoners he sent me to that place in order that I would now return to preach to them. How can I deny the love that God has for our brothers and sisters in prison? What would I do with Hebrews 13:3, which says, "Remember those in prison as if you were there with them, and those who are being maltreated, because you are vulnerable too." Or the words of our Lord Jesus, who said, "I was a prisoner and you visited me." For this reason, despite all of my own needs and those of my family, I cannot stop going out to the prisons – I know that he owes nothing to anyone and that in his time he will repay me – either here or in the next life.

I must express my thanks to all of the people who were praying for me and for my freedom. If I am free today this is the fruit of your prayers, so thank you for the love you showed for me in Christ. Now that I have enjoyed this blessing I would like to ask you a favour – please continue to pray for those brothers and sisters in Christ who are still inside.

# CSW, AND PEACE AND HOPE

## The work of CSW in Peru

Christian Solidarity Worldwide has been involved in Peru for over 20 years. CSW's involvement in Peru has consisted mostly of supporting (spiritually and morally as well as financially) two Peruvian Christian human-rights organisations: the Evangelical *Paz y Esperanza*, or Peace and Hope, and the Roman Catholic CEAS (the Episcopal Commission for Social Action). These two organisations have been at the forefront of human rights in Peru for two decades, fulfilling the biblical mandate to speak out for justice and on behalf of the oppressed. They have done this with little support from within Peru and, regrettably, with only some support from the church (both Catholic and Evangelical) itself. The two organisations work together and both continue to attempt to inform and mobilise the Peruvian church to take the initiative in being a "voice for the voiceless".

## Peace and Hope

"Peace and Hope" is a civil association rooted in the Peruvian Evangelical-Protestant community. Its main objective is to contribute to the transformation of people and society in order to achieve a quality of life which corresponds with God's intentions.

Our work focuses on the promotion of justice and the development of the poor.

We were founded on 19th January 1996 by a group of professionals, pastors and members of various evangelical churches. We have ample experience in the area of attending to victims of political violence and injustice, in prison ministry, in human-rights education, in the promotion of sexual health and in advocacy.

Our services are inspired by Christian principles and by the church's conviction of social responsibility for our country.

We work for people in situations without defence. Impoverished communities in urban areas, ethnic minority communities, social groups and church leadership require our services. More specifically we assist the following individuals or groups.

- Imprisoned people
- Men, women and families who have been victims of political and power abuse
- Children, youths and adults who are victims of sexual abuse
- Female victims of domestic abuse
- Grass-roots organisations
- Local, regional and national authorities (governors, police, judges, prosecutors, mayors, etc)
- Minority ethnic groups
- Church leadership

Peace and Hope contributes to solving the following problems:

- The scars of political violence in Peru (innocent men and women in prisons accused of terrorism, disappeared people, thousands of extra-judicial executions with no resolution, victims of torture, lack of compensation for victims of political violence) and the need for a process of truth and reconciliation.
- Prison conditions which degrade human dignity.
- Discrimination in terms of access to justice, denial of due process, abuse of authority, torture and pressure on victims, especially towards women.
- Continuing conflict between indigenous communities and settlers in Alto Mayo. Little access to justice for the Aguarunas communities.
- Strong social and gender exclusion that at times expresses itself as sexual violence against women and children.
- Repressive sexual culture. Gender stereotypes that asphyxiate sexuality and exclude women. High rates of teenage pregnancies.
- Lack of policies and mechanisms to protect children and youths in terms of their human rights at home.
- A culture of violence. Conflicts are either not resolved or are resolved by the infringement of human rights.
- Marginalised populations are ignorant of, and therefore unable to defend, their fundamental rights.
- Rooted political centralisation and therefore a need for decentralisation.
- Weakening of democracy and institutions.
- Miminal public presence of the church and its participation in social issues. The Protestant Church is weak on social action. Lack of information in churches on models of service and social action.

- Evangelical leaders and organisations from the Andes Region are unaware of the advocacy strategies.

*Our Services*

Mispat – access to justice and pastoral care for victims
  Our Objectives:

- To defend the human rights of marginalised individuals and populations and those who find themselves in situations without legal defence or justice. We thus hope to improve the administration of justice.
- To contribute to changes in institutions and legal mechanisms that contravene human rights.
- To support people in prison both materially and spiritually, together with their families, in the hope of humanising prisons.
- To contribute to the national process of truth, justice and reconciliation.

Jadak – Christian education on sexuality
  We promote sexual education as an organised and sequential process based on biblical concepts and on human development.

Ceconpaz – reconciliation and the construction of peace
  We aim to contribute to a culture of peace, promoting Christian values that help people to respond non-violently to conflicts, especially through reconciliation.

Transforma – strengthening of social action of the church
  We work in the following areas:

- Qualification in influencing politics and advocacy.

- Programme to train deacons.
- Centre for consultations and assessments of NGOs (non-governmental organisations) and ministries.

Urbana – citizenship and local development

- Education and promotion of participation in citizenship through conferences for school groups, youth groups and churches.
- Programmes to train leaders and authorities to work in the area of local development.

For further information about Peace and Hope, please see our website

www.pazyesperanza.org (includes versions in English, French, and Spanish).

E-Mail: aspazes@pazyesperanza.org